About the Editors

Colin Murphy is a community and peace activist. He was chair of the Glencree Centre for Reconciliation from 1988 to 1995 and is currently a council member and part-time member of the programme team. Colin also does consultancy work with Wicklow Uplands Council on sustainable development issues. He retired from a business career in 1999 and lives in County Wicklow.

Lynne Adair is a co-ordinator of a life-skills programme for early school leavers. She has been involved as a part-time programme worker with Glencree Centre for Reconciliation since 1996. Lynne lives with her daughter Sorcha in County Wicklow.

Colin and Lynne operate a consultancy that offers capacity building services, especially in the peace-building and sustainable development fields. They were co-editors of *Untold Stories: Protestants in the Republic of Ireland 1922–2002*, published by The Liffey Press in 2002.

A PLACE
FOR PEACE

Glencree Centre for
Reconciliation, 1974–2004

Edited by
Colin Murphy
Lynne Adair

The Liffey Press

Published by
The Liffey Press
Ashbrook House, 10 Main Street
Raheny, Dublin 5, Ireland
www.theliffeypress.com

© 2004 Glencree Centre for Reconciliation

A catalogue record of this book is
available from the British Library.

ISBN 1-904148-56-5

Printed in the Republic of Ireland by Colour Books Ltd.

Contents

Preface, Colin Murphy and Lynne Adair vii

Foreword, Brian Cowen, TD ix

Foreword, HRH The Prince of Wales xii

President's Message, Alfie Kane xv

*Supporters of the Glencree Centre for Reconciliation,
1994–2004* xvii

Introduction: Thirty Years of Reconciliation, Colum Kenny 1

Fran Banks 8

Máirín Colleary 12

Denis Cooke 17

Geoffrey Corry 22

Philip Crampton 40

Paddy Crean 44

Brendan Crowley 48

Jennifer de Paor 51

Mark Durkan MLA 58

Denis Greene 61

Ali Helimeh 65

Brendan Henderson 68

Marcus Hopkins 73

Liz Iwaskiw 77

Margaret Joyce 81

Isobel Kane 86

John Kelly 91

André Lascaris 96

James Edward Hazlett Lynch 100

Paddy Joe McClean 108

Enda McDonagh 113

Colin Murphy 118

Paul Murphy MP 126

Sean Nolan 129

Sean O'Boyle 132

Una O'Higgins O'Malley 135

Ivo O'Sullivan 139

Frank Purcell 147

Stephen Rourke 152

John Shiels 155

Sonja Tammen 159

Melanie Verwoerd 163

Wilhelm Verwoerd 166

Ian White 176

Preface

In editing this book, we have sought to tell the story of the first 30 years of the Glencree Centre for Reconciliation through the voices of some of those who have been involved in the organisation or who have participated in its programmes.

For reasons that we don't understand, peacebuilding has always been a "minority sport" in this part of the world. How can it be that something as important as the management and transformation of conflict on the small island of Ireland is left to so few? Whilst *A Place for Peace* does not attempt an answer to this fundamental question, it does offer the reader some insight into the experiences of those who have facilitated and engaged in peace-making in Ireland in the past 30 years.

We wish to acknowledge the support of Glencree Council in preparing the book and thank each of the contributors. We are especially indebted to Minister Brian Cowen TD and HRH The Prince of Wales for their forewords to the book, to our President, Alfie Kane for his message, and to Dr Colum Kenny for his introduction. We thank Paul Martin Communications for the cover illustration, Margaret Murphy for back-office support and our publisher David Givens at The Liffey Press for his patience, understanding and guidance.

We wish peace and freedom to all who read this book!

Colin Murphy
Lynne Adair

August 2004

This book is dedicated to all those people who have taken care of Glencree since its beginnings in 1974 and to the many thousands who have worked to build the peace through its programmes and projects.

FOREWORD

Brian Cowen TD

IT IS A PLEASURE FOR ME TO contribute this foreword to *A Place for Peace*, the story of the first 30 years of Glencree Centre for Reconciliation. The facilities at Glencree symbolise and celebrate the immense contribution the Centre for Reconciliation at Glencree is making to the building of lasting peace and reconciliation on this island. The visit of the Prince of Wales in 2002 was symbolic of the increasing understanding and ever-deepening relations between the peoples of these islands.

The very existence of the former barracks at Glencree reminds us that there have been many dark and troubled times in our shared history. But the fact that these self-same buildings are now playing such a central and positive role in the forging of new relationships between us points also to the immense human capacity for change and transformation.

Those of us who have been working at a political level to secure the full implementation of the Good Friday Agreement — in particular the two sovereign Governments — know only too well that, however important the work of establishing new constitutional principles and building new political institutions, the real potential of the Agreement lies in its offer of a new beginning. We will not have achieved its vision of a society dedicated to equality, reconciliation, tolerance, and mutual trust, in which the rights of all are protected and vindicated, until we have effected change in the hearts and minds of people.

That is why the work of Glencree is so vitally important and so deeply appreciated. In facilitating dialogue in its workshops and seminars, in working towards greater understanding, in helping to bring healing to the victims and survivors of conflict, Glencree is playing a critical role in opening up the new dispensation to people and in making change on the ground a reality.

The Government is very pleased that, in addition to our continuing support to Glencree through the Reconciliation Fund, we have been able to contribute over €2.5 million towards the renovation of the former barracks building — now, most appropriately, renamed "The Bridge" — which will be used to advance relations between the peoples of these islands.

All supporters of the Good Friday Agreement would rightly acknowledge the remarkable progress that has been made since it was endorsed by the people of the island, north and south. Measures to ensure a vibrant human rights and equality culture have been put in place. A new beginning in policing is well advanced. A historic step in the decommissioning of paramilitary weapons has occurred. Important first steps towards the normalisation of security in Northern Ireland have also been taken. We have all come a long way.

But there is still a journey to travel yet if we are to fully realise the Agreement's vision. After decades of conflict and division in which great wrongs were done and deep hurts inflicted on all sides, there are many for whom feelings of personal loss and regret will always be strong and keenly felt. Our journey towards reconciliation and rapprochement will, necessarily, be difficult and sometimes painful. In it, we will all have to confront the realities of our past. But in doing so with honesty, and without recrimination or rancour, we can strengthen and enhance the overall healing process.

We will also, of course, have to learn to look forward in partnership and hope together. As the Agreement said, the best way through which we can honour the victims of the conflict is through dedicating ourselves to the creation of a better future. And, as Martin Luther King once observed, "forgiveness is a catalyst, creating the atmosphere necessary for a fresh start and a new beginning". In this work of healing and reconciliation, Glencree will have a continuing and important role to play.

Brian Cowen, TD, is the Minister for Foreign Affairs. This is an edited version of the Minister's speech at Glencree in February 2002. Used with permission.

HRH The Prince of Wales

A Long History which has Caused Much Pain

You may not believe me when I say this but, funnily enough it is nevertheless true: one of the reasons that I am so pleased to have this chance to contribute a foreword to *A Place for Peace* is because I have always felt what can only be described as a sense of affinity with the rhythms of the Irish soul, your sense of spontaneity, the respect for the sacred, which seems to be second nature to you: the inner world of the Irish imagination and your love of nature as the theatre of divine presence. For me in many ways the ancient land of Ireland does have a remarkable tradition of cultural and spiritual creativity and it can be a powerful magic for some.

Another reason is that I now have an opportunity to pay tribute to the work of the Glencree Centre for Reconciliation, and I am only too deeply aware of the long history of suffering which Ireland has endured, not just in recent decades but over the course of its history. It is a history which I know has caused much pain and much resentment in a world of imperfect human beings where it is always too easy to over-generalise and to attribute blame.

For over 30 years the Northern Ireland conflict has destroyed individual lives. As the violence careered forward it wreaked havoc, but over the lonely years places like Glencree have never ever given up. They are the quiet places that painstakingly fostered understanding, hope and love. The physical building there symbolises the quiet but strong places in communities and hearts that never let the dream of peace die. Without them the world would lose the tissue of what is truly humane.

We need to remember that the underlying meaning of peace is not just the absence of conflict; it is equally a climate in which understanding of others goes beyond caricature and where frozen images of hatred and negativity yield to a new vision of shared values and goodness.

If I may say so, it is also especially heart-warming for me that in its work with people, not only in Ireland generally but more widely in Britain, Glencree is able to symbolise something of the important link which still flourishes through the huge number of Irish people over the years who have come to work and live in England.

The Irish have made a unique and important contribution to Britain, a wonderful warmth of laughter, spontaneity and imagination.

At the end of the day, we should never forget that our acquaintance has been long and we can turn that knowing into something new and creative. We need no longer be victims of our difficult history with each other. Without glossing over the pain and suffering of the past we can, I believe, integrate our history and memory in order to reap their subtle harvest of possibility. Imagination, after all, is the mother of possibility. So let us then endeavour to become subjects of our history and not its prisoners.

In the family of European states, Britain and Ireland, as friends and neighbours, can be of huge assistance to each other. Together we can help to create a new community where gradually vision may replace crass functionalism; where respect for individuality and the indigenous may replace globalisation; and where the invisible and voiceless ones may be seen and sheltered.

So I am so delighted that through the British Embassy it has been possible to support a number of the programmes in Glencree, and I do hope very much that this assistance to your important work will continue in the years to come.

I took the greatest possible pleasure in declaring open the new facilities at Glencree when I visited in 2002. Incidentally, I was thrilled, as somebody who has a great passion for restoring and converting, that those otherwise derelict and special buildings have been given new lives at the Glencree Centre for Reconciliation.

This is an edited version of the Prince of Wales' speech at Glencree in February 2002. Used with permission.

PRESIDENT'S MESSAGE

Alfie Kane

As the many stories in this book highlight, Glencree Centre for Reconciliation has been the very heart of a drive to create and sustain the peace process in Ireland for the past 30 years. This process has been borne out of and kept alive by the dedication and commitment of so many people. A list of some of these supporters is included elsewhere in *A Place for Peace* but there are others, too many to mention by name. So, we acknowledge the help of all, especially those whose contributions have gone unseen and unacknowledged. Collectively, they have contributed so much to date and yet we and they know that the journey of reconciliation will surely go on for decades to come as the healing process continues.

It has been my honour and pleasure to have had the opportunity during the past ten years to be involved with this wonderful organisation, first as a corporate supporter and more recently as President. On the occasion of Glencree's 30th birthday I take this opportunity to send two simple messages, firstly personally to everyone who has worked to make the Centre possible and secondly to say that Glencree could not continue to be so effective without the ongoing support of Governments, businesses and dedicated individuals. So, please continue to give your generous support in the many different ways that you do. Thank you.

Alfie Kane
President,
Glencree Centre for Reconciliation

Supporters of the Glencree Centre for Reconciliation, 1994–2004

Glencree Business Club

Alcatel Ireland
Arthur Cox Solicitors
Barclays Bank
BDS Security Management
C&C Group
Development Capital
  Corporation
Diageo
Eircom
G&T Crampton
Gallaher (Dublin)
Gensec
HR Holfeld Group
Interface Ireland
Investor Select Advisors
LM Ericsson
National Toll Roads

O2 Ireland
Parc Group
Paul Martin
  Communications
Royal Liver
Siemens
Silentnight Ireland
Superquinn
Technico
Tilestyle
TV3
Ulster Bank
Unidare
Unilever Ireland
Whirlpool Ireland
XL Europe

Institutional Supporters

ADM/CPA EU Programme
  for Peace and
  Reconciliation (PEACE 1
  & 2 Programmes)
Development Co-operation
  Ireland
FÁS Training and
  Employment Agency
International Fund for
  Ireland
Office of the First and
  Deputy First Minister

Soldiers' and Sailors' Fund
The Atlantic Philanthropies
The Department of Foreign
  Affairs
The Ireland Funds
The Joseph Rowntree
  Charitable Trust
The Office of Public Works
Wicklow County Council
Global Volunteers
The International Women's
  Club of Ireland

Diplomatic Representatives

Austria
Australia
Canada
Finland
Germany
Israel
India

The Netherlands
Palestine
Pakistan
South Africa
Switzerland
United Kingdom
United States of America

Thirty Years of Reconciliation

Colum Kenny

Colum Kenny, BCL, Barrister-at-law, PhD, is a senior lecturer in communications and chairperson of the Masters in Journalism course at Dublin City University. A columnist on the Sunday Independent, *his books include a history of Kilmainham and a study of the Sellafield nuclear plant. He is a former member of the Broadcasting Commission of Ireland and a director of the Media Desk, Ireland. Colum Kenny is a council member of Glencree Centre for Reconciliation.*

FOR THREE DECADES, THE MEMBERS of Glencree Centre for Reconciliation have worked for reconciliation both in Ireland and abroad.

Glencree Centre for Reconciliation was founded in 1974 as a response to violent conflict in Irish society, and out of a conviction that there must be a better way than violence and vandalism, intolerance and sectarianism. Located high in the Wicklow Hills, a short drive from

Dublin via Enniskerry or Rathfarnham, Glencree Centre
is a perfect location for peace work. It is a pleasant place
to meet people.

Glencree provides a permanent and practical centre
of excellence, with its range of programme initiatives
dedicated to securing the foundations of peace and reconciliation and to healing both personal hurts and community divisions.

A spirit of commitment to these ideals inspired the
foundation of the Centre and continues to motivate its
varied activities of peace training and peace making.
Following a particularly horrifying outbreak of bombing
in Belfast in 1972, a number of people and groups met in
Dublin to protest against the atrocities being carried out
in the name of Irish people. An ecumenical service to
voice concern for the people of Northern Ireland was
later held in Christ Church Cathedral, Dublin.

However, concern was not enough. Individuals and
peace groups involved soon recognised that reconciliation was the key and that what was needed was a common base from which to spearhead an effective and non-
violent approach to the urgent issues both north and
south. As a result of their determination to act on this
concern, Glencree Centre for Reconciliation was founded.

The oldest structures at Glencree date from the late
eighteenth century, when a military barracks was erected
to deter rebellion. Between the middle years of the nineteenth and twentieth centuries, Glencree was occupied by
a Catholic religious order which ran it as a boys' reformatory. Thereafter, it was much neglected and its buildings
decayed. In 1974, these same buildings at Glencree were
made available by the government and a substantial bank

loan taken out in order that essential works of renovation could be undertaken. Glencree Centre for Reconciliation was officially opened in May 1975. It has been the scene of important events and projects during the ensuing decades. These are too numerous to detail here, but they have been wide-ranging in their scope, including projects in the fields of education, recreation, fund-raising, work camps and hosting the flow of visitors. During the last thirty years there have been many seminars, workshops, special meetings and addresses, and the extent of the concept of peace and reconciliation can be gauged by the variety of subjects covered.

The work goes on. There is a continuous programme of north/south dialogue, peace studies and conflict resolution courses for secondary school students, as well as sessions for those involved in major conflicts in other parts of the world. The latter have included participants from the Middle East, Sri Lanka and South Africa, amongst other places.

At times of crisis, hundreds of families from troubled areas in Northern Ireland have come to Glencree for holidays or shelter. Community leaders, politicians and trade unionists of all persuasions have taken part in seminars and conferences.

Distinguished visitors over the years have included the Rev Michel Quoist from France, Bishop Helder Camara of Brazil, Prime Minister Jean Chrétien of Canada, former president F.W. de Klerk of South Africa and The Prince of Wales.

The present organisational structure and range of activities stem from 1994 when work resumed on the new Wicklow Wing. That facility was completed in 1998. Dr

Mo Mowlam, Secretary of State for Northern Ireland, and Ms Liz O'Donnell, Minister of State in the Department of Foreign Affairs, performed the opening ceremony. Between 1994 and 2004, Ian White played a central role as executive director of Glencree in expanding the range of activities and sources of funding.

In 1994, Glencree facilitated the establishment of the Irish Peace and Reconciliation Platform. In 1997/98, an inquiry was launched into the role of believing communities in building peace in Ireland and the findings published in a report entitled *Imprisoned within Structures?*

During the late 1990s, the Glencree Business Club was founded. This provides an opportunity for the corporate sector to participate directly in supporting peacebuilding efforts through pledging financial or in-kind contributions to the work of Glencree. Many developments in both programme and capital terms would not have been possible without such support from a variety of companies. Foreign embassies have also assisted Glencree by, for example, financing the refurbishment of rooms or supporting fundraising events.

Today, Glencree works all year round to provide a range of activities and services. These involve a tremendous amount of work and effort and keep the centre very busy. They include:

- Political dialogue workshops

- Victims/Survivors Programmes (LIVE)

- Ex-Combatants Programme

- Alternative Dispute Resolution

- Schools and Youth Programme

- Women's Group
- Churches Programme
- Conflict Studies
- International Programme
- Summer Schools
- Exhibitions
- Residential Centre
- Website: www.glencree-cfr.ie

Glencree Centre is a substantial complex of buildings, some of which are reserved for those involved in specific workshops. However, following recent major renovations, that were made possible only by the generous support of the Office of Public Works, special conference and meeting facilities are now available for hire, and a public coffee shop and permanent exhibition area have also been opened. The income from these facilities helps to pay for Glencree's core work of reconciliation and peace-building.

Glencree tries to ensure on a daily basis that certain values are reflected in the way that the organisation works. These values include:

- Volunteerism (participation is always voluntary)
- Inclusivity (the views of all are welcomed)
- Acceptance (a positive way of writing non-judgementalism)
- Respect for diversity (much conflict arises out of difficulties with difference)

- Finding alternatives to confrontation and violence (conventional methods of resolving conflicts have not always served us well).

- Good neighbourliness (respect for the community and countryside ensures good relations with those who live nearby)

It takes many people to make Glencree work. These include:

- Participants (people from around Ireland and beyond who come to Glencree to participate in peace programmes and other events)

- Staff (a small but dedicated team of employees and international volunteers)

- Council (elected annually by the membership)

- Funders (public and private).

Today, Glencree defines its mission as being to:

- Provide services and facilities which are expressly devoted to the building of peace and reconciliation within and between communities throughout Ireland, Britain and beyond

- Offer programmes, space, and services to help deal with conflict in society

- Enhance the understanding of complex relationships on these islands and share experiences of reconciliation with others

- Facilitate the further development of pluralism and multiculturalism

- Contribute to the formation of new relationships and trust-building within and between these islands that lead to the consolidation of peace.

In seeking to achieve its aims, Glencree acknowledges the contributions of all of those people who to a greater or lesser extent have helped it to realise its ambitions and to grow during the past three decades. Only with similar support in the future will the Glencree Centre for Reconciliation be able to continue to provide its broad programme of activities throughout the twenty-first century.

Fran Banks

Fran Banks MPhil was a founder member of Peace '93. Fran was a volunteer facilitator at Glencree in the period 1994/1996 and was programme director from 1996 to 1998.

Images and Reflections

I RECALL WITH AFFECTION AND TEARS the early, heady days in 1994–95, when Glencree's call came again. Those were the days when the water boiler was very likely to run out and the heating system had a mind of its own; when the log fire in the huge grate warmed me body and soul and the higgledy-piggledy couches covered in multicoloured homemade blankets created such a warm ambience, after a long day of workshops, that I was often reluctant to leave at all. The now state-of-the-art barracks building was adorned with vegetation which grew from the eves and the windows of the shell-like building watched, with empty eyes, the hive of busyness taking place in the slightly ramshackle building opposite.

Everyone did everything and everything seemed equally important. There was a tangible closeness, a sense of purpose, of being part of a small team of workers and volunteers who wanted to quietly inch along the process of change on and between the peoples of these islands. For me in those days Glencree really was a place and an ideal and I felt privileged to be involved and part of it all.

Images float to mind of the organic, exciting process which evolved in my early days with the schools peace studies programmes. The nerve-tingling sense of pushing new boundaries with young people, ripe and willing to explore their own prejudices and to reflect upon the world they live in and will inherit. There was the week-long visit to Belgium, with the Glencree Youth Group accompanied by other groups from north of the border. There, the filtered truths of the Great War were unpacked and rediscovered by young men and women; close in age to many of those buried on the fields of Flanders. I remember the hush as two young Meath women planted flowers on the grave of the poet Francis Ledwidge in a freezing fog, scattering snow falling on the field of white crosses, which stretched sadly far into the distance. Afterwards, I recall the all-night workshop, which enabled the tears and pain to erupt and mesh in the young people's heads and hearts as the enormity and reality of these killing fields impacted on them. One young man decided that the army was not for him after all.

In Glencree too I felt the pain of the Unionist identity for the first time. At the end of a political workshop, a young man sat apart, as sunlight flickered behind him in the old draughty hall, and spoke with such heartbreaking eloquence of the plight of his people marooned on this island. There was the earthy and wholesome presence of the amazing Ballysillian women whose outspokenness and courage gave new meanings to truth. Their straight talking, however, often hid the caring way in which they looked out for each other and indeed for all whom, appearing vulnerable, came their way, me included. There were times when the real possibility of my dying of laughter was not out of the question during or after a workshop. I felt very special indeed when one day someone suggested that I might just make the grade, and I became an honorary Ballysillian woman. The Tim Parry Scholarship always had a special place in my heart. This young boy's death and that of Jonathan Ball, caused by an IRA bomb in March 1993 in Warrington, was the catalyst which shook me out of my lethargy with regard to the ongoing conflict. When I joined Glencree, in the aftermath of the spontaneous eruption of feelings here in the south against the violence, I was delighted to be able to work with the Parry family in their courageous journey of understanding. Each year, a group of young people from schools in Warrington, southern Ireland and both communities in Northern Ireland accepted the challenge of spending a week together. The Scholarship was an intense seven-day experience of visits and workshops that involved the RUC, the Army, people from both communities north of the border and included victims and ex-combatants, amongst many others. They also met all the Secretaries of State in Northern Ireland and President of the Republic of Ireland. One year, Mark, a thoughtful, funny, bright young man from a nationalist working-class area in Northern Ireland, began the week explaining why it was necessary for him to become a dead hero. After many difficult challenges throughout the week, as he handed a poem of his reflections to Wendy Parry at the closing ceremony, he promised instead to become a live hero. Today he is a lawyer.

A sombre note was struck too when Sir Kenneth Bloomfield met the southern victims of the violence of the previous thirty years in Glencree one glorious sun-filled day. He listened with real compassion to the pain of all the individual stories, including those of the victims of the Dublin and Monaghan bombings. His findings were included in his report, "We Will Remember Them", at the launch of which several victims met British Prime Minster Tony Blair. For many of the victims and survivors that day in Glencree was the first time they felt that their positions and feelings were truly heard and respected.

There was theatre, glitz and glamour too. The serious theme "From Rebellion to Reconciliation" underlay a two-day women's event that took place in February 1998. The remarkable influence of women in importance positions in Ireland that year included President Mary McAleese. Veronica Sutherland and Jean Kennedy-Smith, respectively British and US ambassadors to Ireland also came. The notion to celebrate this grew in my mind. Many others joined us on the day, including Nobel Peace Laureate, Mairéad Corrigan Maguire, journalist Nell McCafferty, Áine Lawlor of RTE and Sr Stanislaus Kennedy of Focus Ireland. It was particularly rewarding to have the founder of Glencree, the modest, gracious, inspiring Una O'Higgins O'Malley there with us too. In the true spirit of unsung heroes, Geraldine McAleese, who ran the kitchen at that time with a team of volunteers, must be applauded. Over the days she fed and foddered all and sundry and went on to produce a wonderful candlelit dinner for 130 people, as various characters from the past burst into the room and cajoled and sang and captured the spirit and essence and excitement of 1798.

So my memories end, as Glencree grows, prospers and develops year on year. I am glad I had the opportunity to be part of the place and the ideal for a while.

Máirín Colleary

Máirín Colleary was born in Dublin to a family with roots in Kildare and Cork. She was a philosophy graduate at Milltown and married Gordon in Rome in 1970. They have they have three grown-up children: Barry, Conor and Emma. Máirín developed a career around project management and was involved in many major construction developments around Ireland. In 1982 Máirín Colleary began the relationship with Glencree that continues to the present time.

IN 1982 A FRIEND, PAULINE GEOGHEGAN, asked me to join a working party evaluating the buildings at Glencree. Our brief was to come up with answers to some questions: Should the organisation stay there? What potential, if any, did the complex promise? What possible uses could it be put to? What costs would be involved in partial/complete restoration? I have a clear memory of being impressed with the beauty of the setting there on top of the mountain and experiencing a real sense of peace around the place and the buildings, dilapidated though they were.

I worked with Pauline, Anne O'Meara and Colin Murphy at weekly meetings in Bewley's Cafe in Westmoreland Street, Dublin to see what could, if anything, be done. Glencree's acting council found funds for us to commission a feasibility study and business plan from Deloitte and Touche Management Consultants. This report recommended that, due to the historical and cultural significance of the buildings and the beautiful setting, the organisation should stay on the site if at all possible. The report outlined a "three-legged stool" approach to the future development of the site: space for peace-building programmes, residential accommodation and coffee shop/craft centre. (It is worth noting that, 12 years later, significant progress has been made on each of the "legs".)

The next task we gave ourselves was to find some money to fund the implementation of the new plan. I remember going in a small delegation to meet the Minister of Finance of the day, Bertie Ahern, to seek government support for the first stage of the refurbishment process. Paddy Teahon, an official in the minister's private office, facilitated this meeting. We were advised to make our pitch on one sheet of paper and to get to the point quickly! We must have done a good job because the minister promised to put charity funds into the upcoming budget and Glencree duly benefited to the tune of IR£50,000. I was then asked to join the council and to serve on a buildings committee which was charged with the responsibility of spending the £50,000 on the original buildings and youth wing and then taking the project forward on a step-by-step basis as programme needs dictated and funding became available. That process continues to the present day. Ian White was recruited as Chief Executive around this time and I knew immediately that we had captured an extraordinary young man who could take the organisation forward. Ian quickly secured another IR£150,000 from the Ireland Funds for further capital development. I continued my tenure on the council and buildings committee and participation ebbed and flowed with other pressures and interests. Although I was not then involved in the programme activity, I was always convinced that the culture of the place fitted into my own approach to life: do a bit in your own place and make a difference whenever and wherever you can.

In 1998, I was asked to chair a new Glencree project called The Believers Enquiry project which sought to engage church leaders in Ireland in discussions about peace-building. Again, this task resonated with my own experience in the 1970s as one of the founders of the Dalkey School Project, the first integrated primary school in the Republic of Ireland. I thought that the question that had been put to the church leaders by Glencree was both timely and challenging: "What is the role of your church in building peace and who can work with you in that endeavour?" Glencree had assembled an impressive array of people who agreed to sit on a panel that received the church leaders' submissions and debated them in private sessions. It was an eye-opener to me that the hierarchy of the Roman Catholic Church "disappeared" from our sight, with the result that the major religion on the island of Ireland was not officially represented in the Enquiry. We were fortunate, however, to receive many thoughtful, challenging and self-critical responses which we published in 1999 under the thought provoking title *Imprisoned within Structures?*

In 2002, the then Chair, Stephen Rourke, asked me if I would take over from him. "It's a not a big job," he said. "Just a few meetings and keeping an eye on things." How wrong he was! I was hardly settled in the task when Ian White was sidelined by an unexpected heart condition and I was left with the responsibility of keeping the organisation together. I was tremendously impressed that two Council members volunteered immediately to fill some of the gaps left by Ian's absence. For me, these spontaneous offers symbolised the spirit of the place. We managed to hold the place together until Ian was restored to us, but on the basis that he would move to a part-time programme consultant role. We set about recruiting and appointing a new CEO. Unfortunately, the chosen person had second thoughts and withdrew at the last minute. Our president, Alfie Kane, then called me and asked if I would take on the CEO job. I had many reservations and thought deeply about it. I knew it was an issue of managing a change process from Ian's visionary leadership to the next person. I was honoured to be asked and humbled by the offer and I thought that my experience in project management and business generally would be useful. Four months into the job, my feelings are happy and positive. The programme work that is done here is extraordinary. The way people come together to meet the challenges which are confronting society — old ones like nationalism and sectarianism and new ones like social exclusion and immigration — is amazing.

I have recently been encouraged by a meeting with Dr David Stevens, the newly appointed leader of the Corrymeela Community in Northern Ireland. Our two organisations have always had good relationships and I look forward to developing these in the future.

Glencree has set itself some very arduous tasks: asking questions that others avoid and making inclusivity

work even when it means doing business with people
you don't like. These and other issues like, for instance,
the speed of change, the possibilities that flow from immigration to Ireland, etc., present huge challenges to
civil society. In terms of the Irish peace process, it is a
miracle that the Good Friday Agreement has held up.
Whilst I worry about the ability of extremists to take up
the running again, I believe that civil society will save
itself from more chaos and that Glencree will continue to
play its part in the tricky work of reconciliation and
peace-building. I am privileged to have a part in that
endeavour.

Dennis Cooke

Dennis Cooke was born in Grenada, West Indies in 1938, the son of missionary parents. He was educated at the Methodist College Belfast, the Queen's University of Belfast, Edgehill Theological College, Belfast and Lexington Theological Seminary, Kentucky, USA. He was awarded the Doctor of Philosophy degree at Queen's University in 1980. Ordained in 1965, he has served as a Methodist minister in both the north and south of Ireland. He was principal of Edgehill Seminary, Belfast from 1984 to 2004. He is author of Persecuting Zeal: A Portrait of Ian Paisley *(Brandon Press, 1996) and* Peacemaker: The Life and Work of Eric Gallagher *(Methodist Publishing House, 2004).*

EVEN AS A TEENAGER AT boarding school — the Methodist College, Belfast — I had been curious about the divisions between Christians, especially the division between Catholics and Protestants. It seemed irreconcilable with what I understood of Christianity.

On a Saturday, I would occasionally go on a walkabout in the area of St Mary's Church at Chapel Lane, walking into the church, reading the leaflets in the entrance porch, and strolling in its garden.

I was curious about the Mass. What happened at Mass? What was Roman Catholic worship like? I decided that the only way to find out was to attend Mass one Sunday morning.

So, as a 15-year-old, I walked out the front gates of "Methody" early one Sunday morning and headed for the Church of the Good Shepherd at Ballynafeigh. In my ignorance I was unaware of St Brigid's Church close by. I returned from Ballynafeigh in time for College Breakfast at 9.00 am and was surprised to hear the master on duty announce that he wanted to see Cooke at the end of the meal. When I dutifully enquired what he wanted of me he asked, "And where were you going at 7.00 this morning?" I decided to tell the truth but he wouldn't believe me!

In 1960, as a 21-year-old, I offered myself as a candidate for the ordained ministry of the Methodist Church in Ireland. I had just graduated at the Queen's University of Belfast. The Church sent me out as a pre-collegiate probationer to a country appointment in Northern Ireland. To my astonishment the Roman Catholic curate, Edward Daly, resided in "digs" in the same lane in the town. He was basically doing the work of two men because the parish priest was in poor health. I was appalled by the fact that we never spoke to each other; instead, we simply exchanged the occasional friendly salute.

I asked him into my digs for coffee. Within hours, the story was round the town that the Methodist probationer and the Roman Catholic curate were on very friendly terms, having coffee in each other's digs. A few days later I learned that a Special Quarterly Meeting of the circuit had been called to enquire into what I was teaching about relationships between Protestants and Catholics.

Seven years later, after completing my training in the Edgehill Theological College, Belfast, ordination, and further circuit experience, I was posted as a young married minister to a seaside town in Northern Ireland. The outbreak of the Troubles made life difficult for everyone, especially those most closely affected by them in Belfast. Clergy and lay in the seaside town wondered what they could do to alleviate the suffering of some who had been made homeless. It was decided to offer free seaside accommodation to mothers and children from the Falls and Shankill Roads in Belfast.

Because of my involvement in this cross-community group — it still exists today! — I found myself summoned to another Special Circuit Quarterly Meeting of the Church, this time gaining a massive vote of confidence at the meeting.

In 1971 I was posted to the Centenary Church in Dublin. Because of a fire which had destroyed the premises at St Stephen's Green, the Methodist congregation moved to Leeson Park to share in a joint venture with the local Church of Ireland congregation.

Soon after my arrival in Dublin I was contacted by Ivo O'Sullivan. He invited me to meet with a Catholic-Protestant lay and clergy group who were discussing what they could do to promote reconciliation in Ireland. I responded warmly to this invitation. The names of the group are well known in Glencree because we all became founder members of the new Glencree Centre for Reconciliation. It included Ivo, Una O'Malley O'Higgins, Judy Hayes, Lady Wicklow, John Morrow, Frank Purcell and Shaun Curran.

Sharing with this group was a godsend for me because I was brought into contact with like-minded folk who want to reach out across the divided community and seek healing from the effects of past and present wrongs and hurts. These people were enthusiastic, well informed about the situation in Ireland, north and south, and committed to doing practical things to encourage reconciliation.

Prior to meeting with this Dublin group I had felt somewhat battered by the experience of the two Special Quarterly Meetings. I had asked myself: was working for reconciliation always going to result in rejection and condemnation?

So I owe a lot to Glencree. The community encouraged me, strengthened me, and confirmed me in the rightness and necessity of reconciliation work. I will always be grateful to Ivo and the others I met.

I had to leave Dublin in 1977 and various factors meant I had less time to attend Glencree. But I have continued in reconciliation work. As Principal of Edgehill Theological College, I sought to encourage ministerial and lay students to think seriously about the sectarian nature of Irish society. I ensured that every Methodist ministerial student learned about the teaching of the Roman Catholic Church from a priest and not "secondhand" from a colleague or myself. Seminars were arranged for this purpose. When going on mission teams to various parts of Ireland, I suggested to our local hosts that it would be useful for us to meet with local people from the community, both Catholic and Protestant. One week in Armagh included an afternoon spent in the company of the late Cardinal Tomás Ó Fiaich! He was generous with his time and friendship.

In 2001, the College initiated a joint theological course on Tuesday evenings with the Mater Dei Institute in Dublin, called "Exploring Theology Together". The

course is based on the QUB Bachelor of Theology sylla-
bus. Teaching is 50:50 Roman Catholic and Protestant.
Students are from both communities. It has been an exciting experience. And it makes sense!

Over the years I have learned that reconciliation
work is not easy. Indeed, the personal pilgrimage in
reconciliation is difficult. It is not easy to forgive others
and to learn from others. That is where Glencree comes
in. I possibly made the mistake of not keeping my
contacts with the community. I needed and still need
those contacts. Glencree gave me reassurance. Thanks!

Geoffrey Corry

Geoffrey Corry is an independent specialist in conflict resolution, facilitation and mediation in a number of settings: workplace and business disputes, the Irish peace process, community and family mediation. He has acted as facilitator for over 40 Political Dialogue Workshops held at Glencree since 1994 and was chairman of Glencree Centre for Reconciliation from 1982 to 1987. He trains mediators and has served as chair of the Mediators Institute Ireland, the professional association of mediators in Ireland. The first 20 years of his professional life were spent as a senior manager in youth work with the National Youth Council and National Youth Federation.

PART 1: POLITICAL DIALOGUE WORKSHOPS

Interactive Political Dialogue: A Process that Makes a Difference

I FIRST JOINED GLENCREE IN 1976 when I took over the Methodist "seat" on the Council from Rev Dennis Cooke, who served as Glencree Chairman. At that time, the Council was composed of informal representatives of the Protestant churches in Dublin and various peace groups. I missed the early days of Glencree because I was working in London. Being a Dublin Methodist gave me a good insight into the mindset of the Northern evangelical Protestant, which I had experienced at church meetings in Belfast, and the daily realities of liv-

ing in southern society still somewhat dominated by a
triumphalist Roman Catholic mindset. So my upbring-
ing positioned me well to be a mediator and facilitator.
The first big Glencree event I attended was a Council
weekend in June 1976 to try out the newly opened lower
building at Glencree. I can remember assisting Frank
Purcell, Programme Director, in running the event. The
revamped facility included a new kitchen and dining
area, simple bunk bedrooms and a large hall which
turned out to be rather draughty and noisy. Yet it was
nirvana to all who had worked hard over the previous
two years in fundraising to convert the old Reformatory
buildings into a dream peace centre.

Early Programme Initiatives

I immediately got involved in the programme committee
to run things like the annual Peace Week held around St
Patrick's Day and other peace education events. The big
challenge was how to encourage political discussions on
finding a way out of "the Troubles", the term most in
vogue to describe the Northern Ireland conflict. In 1979–
80, Judy Hayes and I worked with Corrymeela to produce a high-level conference with leading political scien-
tists to explore federalist and consociational forms of
democracy as a way of including majority and minority
identities.[1] We explored whether there was an alternative
to the simple Westminster majoritarian model where a
significant minority was not permanently excluded from
meaningful political participation. Again when the UDA

---

[1] The conference papers were subsequently published in Desmond Rea
(ed.), *Political Co-operation in Divided Societies*, Gill and Macmillan (1982).

produced their "Common Sense" document proposing an independent Northern Ireland within the European Community as a political solution, we arranged a seminar at Glencree to bring them into contact with leading thinkers in the Republic. When Unionists refused to meet with the New Ireland Forum 1983–84, we arranged an unofficial session at Glencree so that they could hear the unionist voice. With Una O'Higgins O'Malley, we had two "Walks of Remembrance",[2] to the Four Courts and the GPO to remember all victims of violence in the Irish conflict as well as the Great Wars, a concept very much ahead of its time.

Despite these modest successes, by the time we hit the mid-1980s I can only seem to remember going through periods of frustration and hopelessness. They were the dark years when we seemed to be getting nowhere. With hindsight, I can see a number of reasons. Part of the problem was the constant funding crisis, which never gave us the professional capacity needed to put our very idealistic projects into action. We were forced to close down the Centre in 1988. Secondly, we were following our collective nose on how to do peace work and to live up to that illusive goal of reconciliation we had set ourselves. Corrymeela and Iona had been our inspiration, but we did not have the advantage of conflict resolution theory so readily available today. Framework models like the Peace Process Architecture[3]

---

[2] See a more detailed account in *The First 10 Years of Glencree*, booklet published by the Glencree Centre for Reconciliation (1984).

[3] This is my own framework based on the concepts developed by several authors: Bill Zartman, Moty Crystal and International Alert.

(see diagram below) did not exist at the time and it could have given depth and direction to our work had we known the difference between the three phases of a peace process. In effect, we were stuck in the "red zone" dominated by the spiral of violence and did not know how to get out of it.

Architecture of a Peace Process		
1. Conflict Management	**2. Conflict Resolution**	**3. Conflict Transformation**
Pre-negotiation phase	*Negotiation of a political settlement*	*Post-conflict phase*
The Red Zone	*The Blue Zone*	*The Yellow Zone*
Acts to break out of tit-for-tat cycle of violence on the ground and move toward a mutual ceasefire so as to allow discussions for a political way out of the conflict	Acts to change the reality of the conflict through creating "talks about talks" and then the negotiation of new political arrangements to remove the causes of conflict	Addresses problems of implementing the negotiated settlement. Transforms the relationship between former enemies through political healing and truth work

Yet we now know that the years 1985–94 were a turning point in the emerging Northern Ireland peace process.[4] Behind the scenes, each side recognised that neither side could win through a military solution — that moment of

---

[4] For a more detailed picture of the behind the scenes negotiations, see Ed Moloney, *A Secret History of the IRA*, Allen Lane: The Penguin Press (2002), Chapters 7–9.

mutual hurting stalemate which Bill Zartman[5] has popu-
larised. From that came a new political momentum between the nationalist parties and the Irish Government
which created the supportive political environment for
the IRA ceasefire.

Interactive dialogue process

My own frustration led me in new directions. I spent
two months in South Africa in 1985 and was introduced
to the Centre for Inter-group Conflict, the mediation
work of Herwe van der Merwe and the emerging concepts of interest-based negotiation borrowed from the
Harvard Negotiation Project.[6] I was inspired by the
strong theological critique of apartheid made by the
South African Council of Churches. This led me to do
mediation training in San Francisco. Then Hugh
O'Doherty (former Glencree staff) introduced me to Professor Herb Kelman at Harvard and Nadim Rouhana
who had brought Palestinians and Israelis together in a
number of problem-solving workshops. All these experiences prepared me for the next stage of reconciliation work at Glencree.

Clearly political dialogue is the key to resolving conflict but you have to change the traditional adversarial

---

[5] William Zartman, "Ripeness: The Hurting Stalemate and Beyond",
in Paul C Stern and Daniel Druckman (eds.), *International Conflict
Resolution After the Cold War*, National Research Council: National
Academy Press (2000).

[6] See Roger Fisher, William Ury and Bruce Patton, *Getting to Yes: Negotiating Agreement without Giving In*, Penguin USA (1991), second
edition.

debating format. There is an old Native American saying: "You talk and you talk and then the talk begins." In
a deeply divided society, it may take two or three rounds
of listening before the real engagement takes place. If the
facilitator ignores the power of the demonising process
or underestimates perceptual barriers and pervasive
fears, they do so at their peril. Without hearing and ac-
knowledging the group story and the underlying concerns and fears, dialogue does not go very far.

Secondly, facilitators need to assist parties to understand the difference between positions, interests and
needs. By moving them into a dialogue about underlying interests and needs, there is more scope for parties to
come to a deeper understanding and joint analysis of the
nature of the conflict. Thirdly, Herb Kelman's work[7]
shows the vital role that mutual reassurance plays in
building positive spirals of mutual trust. If meetings are
held in private under Chatham House rules of confidentiality, over a number of days and at a residential venue
away from the glare of publicity, then there is more
prospect of not only parties having more clarity about
their own perspective on the conflict but also having
greater understanding of their opponent's perspective.
We now know that interactive dialogue goes one step
further. It enables one side to learn how to influence the
other side by responding with political proposals that

---

[7] Herbert C. Kelman, "Experiences from 30 Years of Action Research
on the Israeli-Palestinian Conflict" (2002), www.pon.harvard.edu/
news/2002/kelman_peacemaking.php3. See also Nadim N. Rouhana
and Herbert C. Kelman, "Promoting Joint Thinking in International
Conflicts: An Israeli-Palestinian Continuing Workshop", *Journal of
Social Issues*, 50/1 (1994) 157–178.

incorporate the other's needs and concerns. When each
side is convinced that the other is sincere in its commitment to negotiate a political solution and has the necessary political leadership to deliver it, then we get a
quantum leap into the "blue zone" of conflict resolution.

Reopening of Centre in 1994

It was a happy day after six years of reorganisation
when we cleaned away the cobwebs at the Centre and
got the beds back into shape in time for the first Glencree Summer School, held towards the end of August
1994. It was a seminal event for us because within days
came the republican ceasefire, followed two months
later by the loyalist ceasefire. This changed the political
environment and took us out of those long years of conflict management, making it possible for real inclusive
political dialogue to start at the micro level.

Initially, we invited a group of young unionists who
had attended the Summer School to sit down with
young politicians from Fianna Fáil and Fine Gael. The
next weekend we invited young members from SDLP
and Sinn Féin to meet with the southern parties. To
complete the circle, we brought young politicians over
from British Labour, Conservatives and the Liberal Democrats to meet with southerners and unionists at one
weekend, followed by another weekend when they met
republicans and nationalists. In this organic way, from
month to month, we built a weekend dialogue process
from the needs of political activists who wanted to meet
with each other to discuss current issues in the slow
movement towards political negotiations. In the first few
years from 1994 to 1998, it was not possible to have Ul-

ster Unionists in the same room as Sinn Féin. It fell to southern and other parties who had been present at one weekend with the unionists to convey political messages to the Sinn Féin participants at the next weekend.

Overall, 40 Political Dialogue Workshops have been held in the eight-year period from the autumn of 1994 to the end of 2002 at the Glencree Centre. Participants have come from all the political parties in Ireland and Britain at different times and in different combinations. There have been local councillors, policy advisers, party executive members, officers of youth/women's sections and occasionally some parliamentarians. They were all at the sub-leadership level (see diagram below),[8] mainly because it was more possible for less busy people to come away for a whole weekend and to be free to engage in an unofficial dialogue exercise. It was also useful having officials from the British and US embassies in attendance along with the Irish Departments of the Taoiseach and Foreign Affairs. They were often able to update the group on the way the three governments were thinking but they always felt they learnt more from the participants because they got to see in an interactive and relational way the real nature of the conflict being played out in the room and the road-blocks that had yet to be overcome.

Typically, each residential workshop ran from Friday evening to Sunday lunchtime and brought together about 12 to 15 participants, occasionally going up to 30 people or more when all three strands were present

---

[8] My version is based on the work of John Paul Lederach (1997), *Building Peace: Sustainable Reconciliation in Divided Societies*, United States Institute of Peace Press, p. 39.

(Britain, Northern Ireland and the Republic). Participation has always been open; so at any one workshop, we would have had a few newcomers, some of whom were coming back after an absence and then usually a core group who became regular attendees. Occasionally, we tried a bi-lateral workshop between two parties or between pro- and anti-Agreement voices.

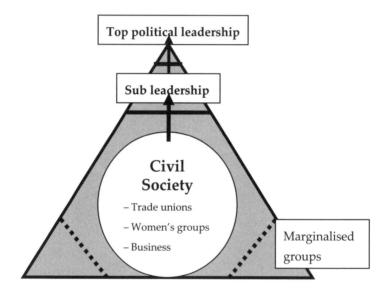

The hallmark of each Glencree workshop was interactive dialogue. The facilitative style was low-key and non-directive. We have always insisted that participants within each workshop decide their own agenda. The best workshops were those which connected people at times of crisis in the lead-up to the Belfast Agreement in 1998 and at difficult stages in the implementation process of the Agreement. We did not put any pressure on participants to come up with solutions or to reach collective conclusions. Some people may see this as a weakness but we always felt that dialogue should remain the focus because of the need to build relationships based on trust. Sometimes a workshop came up with proposals that were written down because of the need to have clarity. Nearly always, participants took away their own personal outcomes or brought back their new insights and new understandings of the other's changing political positions to their respective parties.

Another hallmark was the informal seating arrangements around the fire and the informal time spent together, often into the small hours of the morning, where people got to know each other at an intimate interpersonal level. Probably, we have underestimated how important it has been for people to tell each other their own personal story about the significant events and values in their life which have changed them politically or motivated them to engage in the peace process. Many times as facilitators we have encouraged these moments to be shared in the formal dialogue process but I have no doubt that there were things that could not have been shared in the open group but were shared privately in the corner over a few drinks. We may never hear those stories but they certainly helped people to hear the concerns and fears of the other community and to be more able to reveal their own thinking either informally over dinner or perhaps later on when they were more ready to explore issues in the open session. We always found that the Saturday afternoon and Sunday morning sessions were different. They were more reflective, analytical and interactive, with participants more able to hear each other.

As a facilitator of dialogue, I had to remind myself constantly how difficult it can be for some politicians to engage with each other in the same room or even to come to a workshop. There were times when the peace process regressed and we had to remind politicians of the risks some faced in being seen to be talking with "the enemy" even at the mountain venue of Glencree, away from the public gaze, within anonymity ground-rules. Once or twice a politician left the room, fearing their own life could be in danger when they went back home.

What Did the Workshops Achieve?

It is difficult to assess the impact that this modest civil society initiative has had because of the difficulty of tracking personal change or how relationships which have built up over a series of workshops have actually impacted on political change.[9] At a very basic level, they enabled individual party activists, who became increasingly influential within their parties, to get away from the hectic round of meetings, to relax and recover a bit of thinking space for themselves. We know it helped them to regain political hope that there was, after all, a political way out of the cyclical violence. It certainly enabled them to see more clearly the constraints each party or community were under. As political friendships developed across the divide, lines of communication were opened up between themselves, giving each other access to private phone numbers and e-mail addresses. Even

---

[9] See the two evaluation reports on the political dialogue workshops: Sean McGearty for the years 1994–97 and John Shiels and Peter McEvoy, 1998–2002.

though some of them did not have a direct line into the leadership of their respective party, the workshops also helped participants to explore and bring new light on the difficult issues that acted as roadblocks in the peace process at different points

We thank our funders who made it possible for Glencree to offer residential workshops regularly and consistently one after the other, say every two months, over those eight years. I believe it was this consistency which made the workshops an ongoing unique space in these islands and deepened the peace process at the sub-leadership level. In a couple of years' time, people will no doubt be asking: "Why did it take so long? What was it all about in the first place?" It happened because some politicians took the time to listen to each other and put a lot of personal energy in finding workable joint political solutions.

* * *

PART 2: *THE STEEL SHUTTER*

Impact of *Steel Shutter* Film on the Beginnings of the Glencree Centre

IN 1972, THE IRISH JESUITS HELD a number of simultaneous intensive one-week encounter groups at Rathfarnham Castle in Dublin for some of their own members, to give them an experience in interpersonal relations and group encounter. They were facilitated by Pat Rice (then a Jesuit priest), Bill and Audrey McGaw, all of whom had been trained by Carl Rogers, the influential psychotherapist, at his Center for the Studies of the Person in La Jolla, California.

At one of the workshops, in August 1972, Bill McGaw showed his film *Because That's My Way* and the Irish Jesuits were strongly moved by it. In a conversation afterwards, they wondered whether such a film might be made focusing on the situation in Northern Ireland. Bill and Pat discussed the idea with Fr Cecil McGarry, the Irish Jesuit Provincial, who responded positively. Could such an audacious project ever get off the ground? Where would the money come from? Should North Americans get involved at all? Would Northern Ireland people co-operate?

While the Jesuits supported the film, they decided it would be better for the Center for the Studies of the Person to do it on their own. Carl Rogers made a substantial financial contribution, which, together with other fundraising in Ireland and the US, made production possible. However, one of the Jesuits who had participated in the workshops, Fr Shaun Curran, volunteered to get involved, because of his film-making experience gained at Kevin Street College of Technology. Shaun was subsequently to become an associate producer with Bill McGaw and, when the film was completed, he showed it to various groups in Ireland. That in turn brought him into contact with Working for Peace and led to his decision in 1974 to live up at Glencree to get the Centre project off the ground.

The film turned out to be a ground-breaking piece of work in a number of ways. First, it provided Carl Rogers with the opportunity to show how you can create a safe space for people to talk openly about their personal experiences of a conflict situation. When that happens, it often leads to new understandings which can wash away suspicions and mistrusts about the other group. Secondly it confirmed a new film genre that viewers now know as "reality TV". Thirdly, it showed how mass media with viewer participation could facilitate conflict resolution and trigger social change. It inspired trained facilitators to replicate the Carl Rogers peacemaking model.

Bloody Friday 1972

The most bloody and turbulent years of the Troubles were in 1971–72. The streets of Belfast saw considerable loss of life and the burning of people out of their houses. Events included Bloody Friday on 21 July when 11 people were killed and 130 injured by IRA bombs. The British military ended "no go" areas in Catholic parts of Belfast and there was rioting on the streets on the first anniversary of the introduction of internment. 1972 was also the year that Prime Minister Edward Heath suspended Stormont and introduced direct rule from Westminster.

So when Pat Rice and Bill McGaw arrived in Belfast in early November 1972 on their mission to recruit ten participants for the studio discussions, representing all shades of opinion, they were entering a very polarised political situation with huge suspicions on the ground about their motives. They realised how naïve they had been when a community worker said to them: "After all, when you guys with names like that meet immediately with the IRA and then with the British Army, do you think anyone from the Protestant side would trust you after that? And don't think they don't know every move you've made." With the community worker's help, they started again and made out a very definite plan, which was close to the final make-up of the group. They chose

nine people — four Catholics and five Protestants, one
of whom was an Englishman and retired army colonel.
The group included extremists and moderates on both
sides, as well as old and young. There were three
women participants. Booking a TV studio became another problem. Both
RTÉ studios at Montrose and BBC studios in London
were out because one or other side did not feel comfortable about going into enemy territory. UTV could not release cameras and a studio for a whole three days. It was
decided to fly the group to the United States and do the
video-taping over a weekend in the TV studios of WQED
in Pittsburgh, Pennsylvania, where Bill knew the staff.

Encounter Workshop

Pat Rice and Carl Rogers facilitated the workshop over
three days, 1–3 December 1972. Unfortunately, Carl had
to leave the group two thirds-way through the weekend
because his wife, Helen, had been hospitalised. Audrey
McGaw took his place and appears towards the end of
the film.

The aim was to facilitate straightforward and open
communication with people on opposite sides of the
conflict in Belfast and to film the group interaction. In
fact, in so far as we see them on film, Carl Rogers and
Pat Rice made very few interventions in the course of
the workshop. People just wanted to be able to talk.
Strange to our ban on smoking in Ireland today, participants were allowed to smoke in the studio.

The workshop opens with each participant saying
what life has been like for them amidst the trauma of
living in Belfast through those very difficult months.

Very soon we hear stories of despair. The bitterness, horror, hopelessness and dehumanisation of continued everyday street violence are expressed. It was on the second day that the group struggled with the intensely personal challenge of whether they would allow themselves to openly express their emotions. Each had learnt not to think too deeply about other people's pain and to control their emotions; otherwise "the tears will roll down my cheeks" and "you'll crack up completely". At one point, one of the participants made a statement about the essence of survival in Belfast which provided the title of the film: "You have a steel shutter that comes down in your mind . . . inside your head . . . the real person's on the other side of it . . ."

This triggered another participant, a school teacher, to reflect on his own painful experiences and how he pulls down a "steel shutter" between his functioning self and the seething feelings within. Otherwise he would go berserk. In a quiet soft voice, he speaks of this inner wild beast: "Yeah, I know myself. I am quite aware of this kind of thing and it scares me to know that it is there . . . because it is violent and emotional and daft. . . . I take long walks and let this thing inside of me talk. It isn't quite the same as human feelings — it isn't quite the same as having a beast inside you — some sort of animal feelings, you know."

Pat Rice, facilitator and psychologist, said: "The steel shutter, while protecting you from extreme reactions, can be dangerous psychologically because you become devoid of any emotion. There is nothing now that can shock you. You don't feel any reactions. You become too conditioned to living with violence."

Editing of Video Tapes

Fr Shaun Curran worked with Bill McGaw to edit down
the 24 hours of video tape into a 56-minute film presen-
tation. It was a mammoth task of editing, working long
hours in the studios. It must have involved difficult decisions of what to leave in and what to leave out. Because the main purpose of the film was to show it in Ireland, some of the best content had to be excluded because it would put the lives of participants in danger.

Glencree Group Inspired

Together with Sean Cooney, one of the participants,
Shaun showed the film to peace groups, churches and
communities in Dublin and Belfast. It was featured in
the 1974 Peaceweek at the Irish Film Centre and inspired
many in the Working for Peace group who were hungry
to develop this kind of work. Carl Rogers made it look
so simple! It motivated people like John Kelly to push
ahead with the project to form a reconciliation centre at
Glencree where this kind of group work could thrive. It
clearly had a major impact on Shaun Curran himself and
he gradually found himself taking on the responsibility
in 1975 of being, in effect, the first Centre Director of the
Glencree Centre. He lived in a caravan in the square of
the old reformatory school with his dog Glen through all
kinds of weather. He looked after all the building works,
the opening of the centre and went on to lead a team of
volunteers to run the centre for almost ten years.

Last February 2004, the film was shown again in the
reconstructed Glencree Barracks building thirty years
later to a mixed audience of founder members, present

volunteers and victims of the Troubles. Amazingly, the film spoke to them directly and brought back memories of the worst days of violence. There are plans to use the film again for educational purposes. Hopefully, in the new post-conflict era opening up shortly, it will inspire victims and ex-combatants of the past thirty years to recover their stories and, with supportive facilitation in the open circle, to enable healing to take place through encountering each other's hurts.

Notes and References

The "Steel Shutter" film (1973), 56 minutes, was directed by Tom Skinner and produced by Bill McGaw with Fr Shaun Curran SJ as associate producer. Available from Center for the Studies of the Person, La Jolla. A copy has been lodged with the Irish Film Centre, Dublin.

In a TV interview with John Masterson in Dublin (1985) transmitted on RTE, "Carl Rogers: Personally Speaking", Carl Rogers spoke two years before his death about the impact of the project on himself.

Patrick Rice, "The Steel Shutter", unpublished Doctoral Dissertation (1978).

Carl Rogers, *On Personal Power: Inner Strength and its Revolutionary Impact*, Delacorte Press (1977), pp 129-133.

Philip Crampton

Philip Crampton was born in Dublin in 1959. He was edu-cated at St Columba's College, Rathfarnham, and at Trinity College Dublin where he received a degree in civil engineer-ing. In 1982, Philip emigrated to Canada, spent five years working for a large construction company in Toronto and re-turned to Ireland in 1987. He re-joined the family construc-tion business, G&T Crampton Ltd., where he is now joint managing director with his brother David.

My connection with Glencree evolved from an invi-tation to the first function of the Glencree Business Club in Dublin Castle in October 2000 at which David Trimble was scheduled to speak. My wife and I attended the event and came away impressed with what we heard about Glencree and saying to each other, "How could we help?"

A few days later came my first "Glencree surprise". Ian White, the chief executive, called me to ask for ad-vice and help on a building project. It turned out that a meeting room at the Centre was in need of remodelling and that Jean Chrétien, the Prime Minister of Canada (whom I greatly admired) would be willing to open the new facility, to be called the Canada Room. The snag was that, in order to fit in with Mr Chrétien's schedule, the job would have to be completed in three weeks! What Ian could not have known, however, was that I took out Canadian citizenship as a result of having lived and worked there after I completed my civil engineering degree. I was very keen, therefore, to see what could be done and, after consultation with my business colleagues, and in spite of the tight timing, offered to provide materials and labour to do the job. We managed to complete the task on time and to everyone's satisfaction and the opening event was a suitably grand affair.

I maintained my connection via the Glencree Business Club and was able to continue to support the organisation and to give advice on construction matters when asked. On my various visits to Glencree I was always impressed with the "busyness" of the place and began to get some sense of the important work being done there on the various programmes that the organisation was developing and delivering. Speaking from a business perspective, however, I sometimes wish that a little more order might be introduced to the place and that there would always be a phone that worked, and someone on hand to answer it when it did!

Then came "Glencree surprise" number two. I got a call from Wilhelm Verwoerd, a programme staff member at Glencree, asking if I would meet him for a "chat". Although I sensed, wrongly as it turned out, that my chequebook was to be the subject of the meeting, I agreed to meet Wilhelm. In fact, Wilhelm wanted to know if I would participate in a ten-day visit to South Africa that Glencree was organising. The participants were to include victims/survivors of the conflicts in Ireland. Some of the group would be ex-combatants (paramilitaries, security forces, etc.) and representatives of "civil society" were also to be invited. The group, 20 people in all, were to undertake a wilderness trek in the bush and live together "in the rough"! My first reaction was to refuse on grounds of time but, on reflection and with the encouragement of family and colleagues who said that I should not pass up the opportunity, I eventually accepted and remain grateful that I did.

For someone with my somewhat middle-class background to have this opportunity was incredible. To meet, travel, live with, look after (and be looked after) by people who had firsthand experience of the violence of the past 30 years — both in terms of handing it out and being in receipt of it — was indeed a privilege. Here I recognise the skill and care with which the trip was organised and the professionalism of Wilhelm and his colleague Jacinta de Paor in helping us to gel and make it all work. I was given new insights into people's motivations in conflict situations and learnt how complicated the picture of our Troubles really is. It's not simply a case of Protestants/Unionists on one side and Roman Catholic/Republicans on the other. I heard about splits that arise when family members find themselves on different sides of a conflict, sometimes with tragic results. Experiences such as these helped me to develop some understanding of the complexities within the broad political and religious traditions and how foolish it is to make sweeping generalisations about one or the other. This realisation has led me subsequently to reflect on the need for people of the Church of Ireland community in the Republic of Ireland (my "tribe") to engage more with their counterparts in Northern Ireland and to develop greater mutual understanding and respect for each other.

So, my experience of Glencree is positive and I am happy that I have been of some use and, at the same time, grateful for what I have learned through my association with the organisation. Apart from all the benefits of the implementation of the Good Friday Agreement in terms of the ending of violence and communal conflict I have always taken the view that peace is good for business. I am happy therefore to support Glencree in whatever way I can and I recommend that anyone who wishes for good sense and pragmatism to prevail in Ireland should do likewise.

Paddy Crean

Paddy Crean was born in Dublin. His father was an Irish army officer, the son of a cabinet-maker from Cork. Paddy spent his entire working life with the Department of Post and Telegraphs, later Telecom Éireann before it became Eircom, where he developed a career in sales/marketing and human resource training. Paddy and his wife Angela live in Wicklow and spend much of their time travelling and visiting their children and grandchildren. Paddy is a convinced peace worker and was involved in the New Consensus and Peace Train initiatives in the 1980s. Paddy Crean was elected chair of Glencree in 2004.

I HAVE ALWAYS TAKEN AN INTEREST in the British dimension in Ireland — as a result of my schooling by the Irish Christian Brothers and the influence of my father, who had joined the IRA at the age of 18 and subsequently spent 18 months of his young life interned at Ballykinler Camp in County Down.

Throughout the 1970s and 1980s I was appalled by the extremes of hatred, bitterness and resultant violence that marked the escalation of the "Troubles" emanating from the disturbed historic relationship between Ireland and Britain. Like many others south of the Border my only reaction to date had been to wring my hands and wish it would only be over — ideally in the form of a United Ireland. The fact that much of the reported violence was perpetrated in the name the Irish people was a matter of deep concern to me. Yet there was nothing I felt l could do to prevent ıt.

My early involvement in peace work arose from my participation in a Buddhist group that exhorted practitioners to exercise compassion by taking action. I seized the opportunity when one Saturday morning I heard on the radio that a group of Northerners were due to arrive in Dublin on a "Peace Train". I immediately proceeded to Connolly Station to shake cross-border hands extended in peace and friendship. Not only that; I boarded the train and joined the return journey to Belfast. Among those I met on the journey were Sam McAughtry and the late Paddy Devlin.

After that experience I became a committee member of the Peace Train Organisation and New Consensus, the group that organised the first Peace Train. It took some deep soul-searching for me to be convinced by my new associates that we should demand as central to building peace in Ireland the amendment of Articles 2 and 3 of the Irish Constitution, which laid territorial claims on Northern Ireland. In addition, we demanded an end to the killing and requested an opportunity for dialogue with the Republican leadership.

Wearing my New Consensus hat, I was one of the seven men who chained themselves to the railings of Kevin Barry House in protest against the killing of seven workmen in their van at Teebane Cross. I later took part in the collection in Dublin and delivery of floral tributes for the victims of atrocities, notably Teebane Cross, Ormeau Road Bookmakers Shop, Greysteel "Trick-or-treat" murders and Warrington.

Heretofore, my actions vis-à-vis Sinn Féin/IRA had consisted of protest. The emerging Hume/Adams contacts indicated to me that the urgent need now was for reconciliation. On the Belfast/Dublin/London Peace Train I had met with two members of the then almost-defunct Glencree Centre for Reconciliation. They told me about its initial actions as a protest group and how they soon realised that a more fruitful path to follow was one of reconciliation. I joined Glencree forthwith.

This was in 1993, when that organisation was re-awakening. Glencree was going through the process of re-establishing its capacity to make a contribution to the developing peace process and I was optimistic that the potential was there to do something useful. I saw myself as a supporter who could work behind the scenes to build the organisation up again.

When Ian White was appointed chief executive in 1993, I immediately saw it as my task to place my complete trust in him and support him in any way I could. I could see that Ian had a vision for Glencree that was informed by a careful analysis of the complexities of the situation that was coupled with boundless energy, enthusiasm, persuasiveness and capacity for hard work. Indeed, I often observed that Ian had a solution ready before the rest of us knew that there was a problem! In this context I had no problem in volunteering to write letters for Ian, attend meetings in his absence and act as a general factotum.

I was elected to council in 1995 and became honorary secretary. I applied myself to managing the membership records and designing and updating a database. In the absence of anyone more qualified I acted as informal IT consultant and webmaster. Despite my self-appointed position as a backroom boy, I found myself getting involved in work with the political dialogue workshops, an activity dear to my heart, and the schools programme. Given the age difference, I withdrew from the latter when we recruited a professional team and new volunteer facilitators.

The values that Glencree espoused when it reopened in 1994 fitted well with my own philosophy of non-aggression, working for solutions through dialogue and finding alternative ways of resolving conflict.

As Glencree has got stronger and broadened its scope in recent times, it is interesting and challenging to observe international interest in its work. I believe that this is due in part to an appreciation of the fact that the Glencree experience has placed us in a unique position in the field of reconciliation.

We were where we were when there was nobody else in sight. Glencree is still there. However, lest we lose the run of ourselves, we would do well to remember the wry comment of an Ulsterman at a session in the Centre: "If it wasn't for the shipyard workers of Belfast, the *Titanic* wouldn't be where it is today."

In 2003, I stood down as company secretary and was recycled as chairperson in 2004.

Brendan Crowley

*Brendan Crowley was born into a farming family in Cork in
1936. After school and university he spent his working life in
horticulture in England and in the Dublin/Meath borders.
Brendan moved to County Wicklow in 1986.*

IN 1986 I WAS WORKING IN THE Dublin/Meath borders
and took an opportunity to visit Glencree. My plan at
that time was to work in Africa but the combined effects
of a road traffic accident and being diagnosed with a
chronic illness caused me to change my plans. Eventually
I went back to Glencree, offered my services as a volunteer and, to my great surprise, find myself still there as a
neighbour and almost-daily visitor, almost 20 years later.

My specific task was to work on the farm that the
Centre owned, and still owns. The 13 acres there were
being developed as a facility that introduced urban-based
children to the countryside in the context of learning to
live in peace with their environment. With the benefit of
hindsight, one can now see that this initiative programme
was literally and metaphorically groundbreaking and
probably 20 years ahead of its time in terms of best envi-
ronmental education practice. My memory is that some
thousands of schoolchildren participated in that programme on a yearly basis.

In those times, the Glencree organisation seemed to be
continually in the grips of one crisis or another. There was

a degree of friction between the Council and the small Centre staff and volunteer team. There was never enough money with the result that people lived and worked at the Centre on a hand-to-mouth basis. Next month's budget always seemed to be spent before we actually received it. I well remember James McLaughlin, the Centre manager in those times, going with Gloria Fralick to visit the honorary treasurer in hospital. (Gloria was a Canadian volunteer who eventually married a local farmer and who now lives in the Glencree valley with their two children.) Their mission was to get a cheque signed to buy food for the staff and volunteers. The patient mistook the appearance of James and Gloria at his bedside as an entirely humanitarian visit. He declared himself so delighted with what he perceived as an act of mercy that James was too embarrassed to produce the cheque and returned to the "nest" with Gloria empty-handed!

The Centre was in those days a much more uncomfortable and grim place that it is today. It was almost impossible to heat the rooms and there were continual problems arising from the generally dilapidated condition of the accommodation. Nevertheless, important work went on there, especially with young people who were prepared to tolerate the Spartan and austere conditions.

In spite of all efforts to avoid the closure in the late 1980s, I have no doubt that this was the only decision that could be taken. Any enterprise has to be able to pay its way in the world and I doubt if Glencree ever did. The decision to close was a courageous one and the success and effectiveness of Glencree today is proof of its wisdom. In spite of not having a specific religious ethos now, I believe that Glencree is a more "Christian" place than it was in earlier times. I can see a level of tolerance around the place that didn't always exist and staff, volunteers, council and members seem to me to be a reasonably happy bunch. The radical improvement in the physical condition of the Centre enables work to be done with all kinds of people and I believe that Glencree has really come of age. To see people live and work here from all parts of these islands, from mainland Europe, the Middle East, Africa, the Indian sub-continent and elsewhere is really thrilling for me. The people on the staff and volunteer teams are of the highest quality and are true heirs of their predecessors who worked under such difficult conditions in the early days of Glencree.

In spite of all the problems, my association with the Centre, starting from those hard times, has benefited me in many ways. I have many happy memories, especially of staff and fellow-volunteers, and I still feel at home when I visit the Centre. As a frequent visitor and self-appointed "father" to each crop of volunteers, it is humbling for me to go there and be aware of the stories of forgiveness, repentance and healing that are facilitated one way and another by Glencree.

I wonder how Penny, a volunteer from New York who worked on the farm in the mid-1980s, would view the place today. I gave her a bowl and sent her into the henhouse to collect eggs. I omitted to tell her that the eggs were destined for the kitchen. She left them outside on the ground and the birds had a feast.

Jacinta de Paor

Jacinta de Paor has been the co-ordinator of the LIVE (Let's Involve the Victims Experience) programme at Glencree for the past five years. Her training is as a psychologist for 20 years, with further training in counselling psychology and psychotherapy. She worked for two years with the Psychology Department at Johns Hopkins University, Maryland, USA. Other experience includes working with the National Training Development Institute's third-level college for people with disabilities and working with a young offenders' institution. She also works with a counselling course which she co-founded ten years ago.

When I was first invited to come to work with the Glencree programme for victim/survivors of the northern Troubles, I wondered what on earth I would be able to bring to this work. I was someone from the south who'd spent her time away from the scene of the conflicts and whose life had been unaffected by the Troubles. I hadn't been injured or lost someone close to me. I did hear one bomb go off but hadn't been close to the scene of the explosion. My experiences of the Troubles in and around Northern Ireland came largely from the images I saw on television. I also had the privilege of being able to switch off that same television if I chose. Those with whom I was about to work didn't have that same option. They were living those experiences daily.

And so five years ago I started my journey with Glencree. But as I worked myself into the job I noticed something else happening. Increasingly I became aware that the northern accents I heard were voicing expressions that were so familiar to me from my childhood. So the familiarity of the North slowly wrapped itself around me. Being surrounded by people telling their stories, I gradually found myself talking more and more about my own northern roots. My mother came from Coleraine but the family had moved to Dublin, bringing their own family secret with them: my grandfather had been a member of the Royal Irish Constabulary, the precursor of the Royal Ulster Constabulary, in the 1920s. When I was growing up I was never to mention this outside the family. We were simply told that people wouldn't understand. Any photos of my grandfather in uniform were always kept hidden and I didn't find them until after my mother died. When I was small I do remember causing a fuss when I found his police baton, which was always kept hidden in a wardrobe! I was brought up to believe that Protestants were the people who had deprived my mother's family of chances to progress in life and yet the paradox was that my grandfather was a Catholic in the mainly Protestant police force. Another paradox we grew up with was that my mother and her sisters had completed their nursing training in England. They often said that England had given them a start in life that neither Northern Ireland nor the Irish Republic had. Yet, when the anthem "God Save the Queen" was played on television, there was a rush to turn it down as it was explained to us that "our Protestant neighbours shouldn't hear Catholics supporting England".

I had spent many hours working out these prejudices for myself. Nonetheless, this was the history that I brought with me when I came to Glencree and I was about to have many of my prejudices challenged further. I found that I was constantly having my own shortcomings, biases and prejudices uncovered by the individuals on the programme. These were the very people whom I had been brought up to believe were different to me. I thought I would be working with their biases rather than with my own! Because the conflict in Ireland was something that affected my own and neighbouring countries, then I was going to meet it on a personal as well as on a professional level. This work was not going to be something that I could remain outside.

However, one thing that I thought might be useful arose from my tendency to question. In other words, I was a bit of a rebel. My previous training in psychology had led me to work with those who were troubled and excluded — people often seen as those to be feared by society in general. These were individuals who had been through prison systems or those who had severe psychological problems. But my driving force was that I always had a desire to meet the person behind the label. The more people I met in these circumstances and the more I listened to their stories, the stronger this desire became. Perhaps this desire to see behind the labels would be something that would help me when I found myself challenged personally.

Initially I was concerned as to what I could offer to those who had experienced the Troubles at first hand. Yes, I had worked with people who had suffered loss and trauma in their lives but never trauma on a scale that affected so many at the same time. I had enough experience to realise that the main support I should offer was to make a space where those experiences could be openly expressed and talked about without questions being asked or explanations demanded. From my work experience I knew that people wanted to be allowed to tell their story without interruption or judgement.

The more I heard, the more humbled I became at how people could survive the events that they had been through. My head told me that often there is no choice for the person other than to keep going but my heart told me that all these events must extract a huge price from the individual.

In developing the LIVE programme, I became involved in helping to create something new and unique at Glencree. We were bringing together groups of individuals who wouldn't meet under everyday circumstances. All had experienced trauma or loss due to the Troubles in Northern Ireland. Many programmes were already doing excellent therapy work in this field but where we differed was that we brought individuals together from all parts of these islands for the purposes of building relations between them rather than for purposes of therapy. (As we would only have people attend the programme at irregular intervals, we felt that their therapy needs were best served on a more frequent basis nearer to where they lived.) Building relationships, we believed, would further peace-building work between our peoples, if each person had a chance to see that there were victim/survivors in all the neighbouring countries who suffered hurt in similar ways.

Further to this, we had requests from participants to meet with former paramilitary prisoners. This presented us with a dilemma because at Glencree our ethos is non-judgemental, receiving all equally. We didn't want to see a situation develop where one group sought to lay blame at the feet of another. Neither did we want to cause further hurt to the group of victim/survivors by being seen to support those who they saw as having caused their suffering. Also, we were aware that by singling out groups in this way we would create situations in which victim/survivors and ex-paramilitaries would be seen as having sole responsibility for the Troubles. In this scenario, everybody else on these islands would bear no responsibility for what had happened. Glencree's view of the "landscape" of reconciliation is, however, that we all share responsibility for what has happened and for the hurt that has been caused. Getting this dialogue going and sustaining it has been and continues to be one of the greatest challenges of our work.

As we got into the work, time and again my memory of the programme is one of a deep sense of love for the people I have met along the five-year journey. I often look round the room on a Saturday evening after a very tough day and see the faces of those who, despite the traumas in their own lives, still manage to make time for, look out for and help each other. How much they appreciate the smallest thing we do for them. At times like this I tell myself how privileged I am to have had the chance to know my fellow humans at this deep level. All the petty day-to-day frustrations, annoyances and worries fade away when I am confronted with such open and generous people. I take heart when I see a participant able to stand in a group of those who, at one time, they would have seen as their opposites and be able to debate and stand up for their own side. More and more the participants have taught me to watch and listen rather than being too ready to spring into action with a neat solution. I have learned that by listening I will learn more than I could by reading any of my academic books about working with trauma. In other words, I have learned to be humble and merely to offer suggestions rather than solutions.

I have also learned the value of working alongside others at Glencree who hold values similar to mine. How strengthening it is to be able to work together towards similar ends. I have rarely experienced a workplace with such a level of support and generosity of spirit. To be in a place that encourages us to actively put into practice the values we promote for those who use our Centre is incredibly refreshing.

But my challenges pale into insignificance when I am faced with those who engage in this work. Time and again I have been inspired by the courage that Glencree has shown. Often Glencree takes steps that others would deem foolhardy and dangerous. I have seen Glencree take risks that often evoke criticism rather than praise. This is when I experience some of my greatest (if toughest) moments in this work. It is often hard to listen when someone criticises what your organisation stands for and puts down your colleagues when participants don't see what goes on outside of programme time. I have often sat through soul-searching staff meetings where these self-same courageous colleagues have openly challenged themselves and their own viewpoints. I try to remind myself that this work is not something that we do to make friends; rather it is about valuing our fellow human beings, whether or not we agree with them. We know they are indirectly paying us a compliment by freely expressing them and criticising us openly. This freedom is something that hasn't always been possible over the course of the Troubles without fear of repercussions.

My hopes for the future of our work here at Glencree lie with the courageous people who come through our gates. Their courage in taking the decision to participate in the first place is something that gives me strength to continue with the work. If, for our part, we can continue to encourage them to be with each other in a spirit of openness and respect, then there is hope that peace will grow in places which have seen so much sadness and hurt.

I get encouragement for the work we do in hearing Glencree highly spoken of outside of Ireland. Yet you will hear those who work here at the Centre stress that we are not "the experts" in the field. This is indeed true, in that we are only one organisation amongst many who have taken up the challenge to do this work. I would hope that our work here will become less urgent and less needed as time goes on. My wish is that in the future our work will, in the main, be preventative and that gradually the need for centres such as Glencree will become unnecessary as reconciliation work is adapted into mainstream curricula and workplaces.

Mark Durkan MLA

Mark Durkan is the Leader of the SDLP Party. Mark was SDLP Chairperson from 1990 to 1995. In 1993 he was elected to Derry City Council. He was one of the Party's Chief Negotiators at the Inter-Party Talks which led to the Belfast Agreement and directed the SDLP's successful Referendum Campaign, securing over 96 per cent support for the Agreement among party voters. He was elected to the Northern Ireland Assembly in June 1998 and was appointed Minister for Finance and Personnel on the Executive in December 1999. Mark was elected Party Leader in November 2001 and became Deputy First Minister of the Northern Ireland Assembly in December 2001.

OVER THE LAST 30 YEARS, the name "Glencree" has grown synonymous not just with upholding the ideals of peace and reconciliation, shared understanding and mutual respect, but often with their fulfilment in the most difficult of circumstances. The change of environment Glencree offers has helped encourage a change in thinking among many who have taken part in its workshops and programmes. I know this is true for many young people from the North who have been able to challenge others, have been challenged themselves and have even challenged themselves as well. This is what Glencree is all about — the opportunity for people to engage with others from different backgrounds, with diverse outlooks but sometimes more in common than we knew in ways they may not otherwise be able to.

The Peace Process has taken many twists and turns in Glencree's lifetime. From the brutality of violence to the sterility of suspension, through the hope of the Good Friday Agreement and referendum, the politics of peace-building has never been easy. None of us ever thought it would be. Speaking at Glencree in May 1983, then Taoiseach, Dr Garret Fitzgerald said: "The work of reconciliation is the greatest single challenge that faces this generation in Ireland. As each of the last ten years has gone by, the task has become more daunting, more complex and more heartbreaking."

Twenty-one years later, we have a full understanding of what Dr Fitzgerald meant. As Glencree celebrates thirty years in the challenge of bringing people together, and six years after the people of Ireland voted for living together, there is a real risk that we in the North will settle for living apart. That was never meant to be the high ceiling of our shared ambition in the Agreement. The fact that things aren't as bad as they used to be must not absolve us from striving to make things as good as they can be. These are the choices we must now face. Do we want to live together or grow apart? Do we want to share power — nationalists, unionists and others working together — or carve power up and settle for working apart? Are we to achieve an ever-more shared society or are we to settle for more peaceable division, uneasy stability and more ordered hostility? I believe we can do better than that. We can bridge community divides, overcome border barriers and keep narrowing the gap between what is and what ought to be.

I am clear: we cannot give up now. Too much has been invested and too much will be lost to us all if we fail to fulfil the Agreement. Over many years, people have come to places like Glencree and spoken openly and honestly about their hopes and their fears for themselves and for their children. Common to all those people is the deep desire for something better. We owe it to all who hold out that wish, as we owe it to ourselves, not just to do better by each other, but to do the best we can with each other and for each other.

As Glencree continues to grow — provoking debate and promoting understanding and respect — I wish it every success for the next thirty years and more.

Denis Greene

Fr Denis Greene was born in Clontarf in 1921. He attended the Catholic University School (CUS) in Leeson Street, Dublin. His was a mixed (inter-Church) family. He intended to join the Civil Service but found a vocation to be a priest with the Society of Mary (Marist Fathers) and was ordained in England in 1947. He taught French as a supply teacher in the post-war period and later went to Downing College Cambridge to read French. He served as headmaster in a grammar school in Blackburn for 25 years. Fr Greene lives with the Marist Community in Dublin.

WHEN I CAME BACK TO DUBLIN in 1975, I happened to take a bus to Enniskerry, intending to walk in the Wicklow hills. A car stopped and offered me a lift and the cheery middle-aged driver turned out to be Fr Shaun Curran SJ, Director of the Glencree Centre. He dragged me into the caravan in which he was living, in the midst of a sea of mud, made a fry-up lunch for me and told me the story of his hopes for Glencree. I came back that summer with students from Chanel College in Coolock where I had taken up a teaching position. The boys joined in work camps that aimed to turn the dilapidated buildings into something remotely habitable. The boys were amused at having to pay to work! It was hard work, conditions were austere and we slept on the barracks floor through freezing winter nights. In spite of the conditions, the young people found that there was a purpose in hard work and this understanding has come back to me again and again. The boys loved going to Glencree, it was something special.

Through my experience of those work camps, I was challenged to dump any ideas that my vocation was to be comfortable. Glencree brought different people close together, with the additional possibility of wiping social distinctions. It was there that I learned the value of listening to the "other".

People from Northern Ireland who came to Glencree at the height of the Troubles were astonishing. I remember overhearing a group of Protestant women from Belfast chatting. One said, "Yon man is a priest, he is very nice. Isn't it a shame those Catholics don't know God." However, the following Sunday, the group turned up at the chapel and one of them said to me, "You're a grand wee minister, will you give me communion?" I was pleased and humbled and told her that I had never refused anyone. However, I asked her to think carefully about the consequences of someone reporting back home that she had gone to Mass and she decided not to communicate. This was a good instruction for both of us and we understood each other. I vividly remember the tears at Connolly Station when we parted. This was a different and worthwhile experience for me, an Irish priest who had lived in England for a long time. One of the things I learnt was never to say things like "Oh my God!" in the presence of Protestants!

I stayed around the place and eventually found myself on the council of Glencree. It was around this time that it began to dawn on me that the culture of the organisation was not as "spacious" as I thought it was. I found there were two councils, a telephone one and the rest of us. Those on the telephone council had time to talk on the phone and make decisions. They were idealists and we needed them. Religious people would call them prophets. Nothing happens without them and sometimes nothing happens with them! Prophets are two steps ahead of the rest of us, they can even see the horizon. Meanwhile the rest of us were trying to unblock the drains!

If I had been courageous, I would have said, "What had you decided before the meeting, just tell us and we'll get on with it". Although Glencree had set out to be an open Christian ecumenical centre in the image of The Corrymeela Community in north Antrim, I don't thing that ever really worked. The Vatican Council and the Pope's visit had happened but true ecumenism just hadn't sunk in. The Glencree Catholics felt that the Protestants were nice people but wondered what they were really for in this Catholic country. Meanwhile, the minority Protestants were all for pluralism and inclusivity, the exact opposite of what happened when they ran the country! I saw all this as tiresome in the extreme.

For me it was a humble ministry of just being there. We must have done some good because occasionally I get a card from a volunteer of thirty years ago and sometimes they even come to see me. These connections mean a lot to me.

In 1982 I was appointed to a position in Rome so I lost touch with Glencree. I subsequently came back to Dublin as novice master in the Marist community — a big job then. I re-established my connection but the or-

ganisation was then beginning to re-define itself and I
became less and less involved. However, I believe that
Glencree was part of my formation and was important
in helping me to understand Protestants and Unionists. I
wanted then what I want now, for all of us to find a way
to share this island — a communion of Christians within
the wider community. The rain falls on us all.

Ali Helimeh

Ali Helimeh was born in the Lebanon. His family moved to Palestine but were forced to leave after the establishment of the Israeli State. He studied literature and languages at the Arab University in Beirut. Ambassador Helimeh joined Fatah, the Palestinian national movement, in 1974 and in 1978 joined the political department of the PLO. Based in Tanzania, he served the Palestinian cause and people in Africa for 25 years. During this time he studied the policies of the ANC, Zanu PF etc. and developed important linkages with them. Ali Helimeh came to Ireland in 2001 to serve as Delegate General in the Palestinian diplomatic base in Dublin. He has used his time there to study the Irish peace process at first hand. Ambassador Helimeh's wife Iman and children Ahmed and Noura live happily with him in Dublin.

MY FIRST CONTACT WITH GLENCREE was in 2000. I found it a very positive place to bring fellow Palestinians and my journey with Glencree started then. Glencree is very useful and important for the Palestinian Delegation in Dublin and helps us strengthen relationships. The organisation was very co-operative in building the bridges that led to the recent visit to Dublin of a joint Palestinian/Israeli parliamentary delegation. Glencree worked tirelessly to make this important event happen. It is amazing how Glencree people were prepared to travel to the hottest areas in the Middle East to make the arrangements for this very positive and hopeful initiative.

I believe that Palestinians can learn from the elements of the Northern Ireland peace that are common to our own situation. The experience we gain here is informing policy at all levels in the Palestinian Authority. We must be willing to dialogue with others about how to manage the divisions that are preventing a political settlement and an end to illegal violence in our region. This is a goal to which I am personally committed, hence my willingness to work with Glencree on any relevant issue.

The Centre is a fantastic resource, constantly extending the hand of experience and friendship. To my knowledge, no other similar NGO exists that is attempting this vital work. I particularly appreciate the meetings that Glencree facilitated with Mr Danny Maggido, the Israeli Ambassador to Ireland. Glencree is an agent for change that must never give up working for positive outcomes to the ongoing Middle East peace process. More ideas could and should be explored and I am grateful for offers of help from the diplomatic community in Dublin. My Delegation is prepared to go further, to work harder for peace in our troubled region and to accept any assistance. We are looking for a win/win solution.

The Glencree location is beautiful and inspiring, The informal way of living with the volunteers creates a relaxed and happy environment that is unique in my experience. The Centre is so different from a hotel or conference centre thanks to everyone being willing to work tirelessly to achieve the organisation's mission to build peace. I have learnt to relax there and to talk freely and openly — and to listen, not least to the important Israelis whom I have met there. Glencree energises me to go further and deeper to explore issues of conflict resolution through dialogue and problem-solving. I wish the organisation well and am looking forward to my next visit. *Salaam eleikum, peace be with you.*

Brendan Henderson

Brendan Henderson was born and reared in Dalkey, County Dublin and now lives in nearby Cabinteely. Brendan was a Fine Gael member of the then Dun Laoghaire Corporation from 1979 to 1991 and was Cathaoirleach (Chairperson) in 1984. With family roots in Belfast, Brendan decided on foot of the developing peace process to work for the improvement of dialogue between the different traditions in the Cabinteely district and those elsewhere who shared a similar objective. This led to his involvement in the Glencree Churches Programme, to which he is totally committed. He describes himself as an avowed pacifist. He is married to Terry and they have an adult family.

My first recollections of hearing the name of this place, Glencree, come from my childhood, 1947 to be precise. The devastating War in Europe was over but its aftermath resulted in many young children, mostly German, coming here as refugees under a project called "Operation Shamrock". One of these young refugees, Ursula Becker from Dusseldorf, was billeted there and subsequently came to stay in my home. Occasional trips to the Wicklow Mountains invariably included a momentary pause at Glencree "barracks", neglected and awaiting the possible fate of eventual demolition.

Later, I read occasional pieces about the development of Glencree Centre as a reconciliation centre. My impression was that some "fine people" had come together to promote peace and reconciliation. Whilst it all sounded great it seemed to me that this was another bunch of well-meaning folk who were wasting their time.

In the early 1970s, through involvement with my parish youth club, I renewed association with "Glencree" but not immediately with the old "barracks". On some of our weekends in the mountains, we visited the Glencree Centre and were given a guided tour of the farm that was now developing in the place. There were pigs and other livestock and much talk about lifestyle changes, etc. I was aware that there was a continuing risk to the future of the Centre because of the obvious high costs of maintaining such a massive facility. I was not surprised when I heard the place had closed down.

Roll the clock forward to 1995. We made contact with Ursula Becker and there was great excitement and joy when she returned to the Ireland she had left in tears in 1949. A trip, with all its possible pain, to Glencree was obligatory but it proved to be a great moment for many reasons. Ursula shared many stories of her time in Glencree and of how harsh the conditions were, especially the cold winter weather. But she also spoke of the great care and love that was lavished on those refugee children.

During all this time other seeds, sown some time earlier, were beginning to bear fruit. Northern Ireland, dear to my heart — my father's birthplace — was seeing the possibility of an end to 35 years of violence. A fragile Peace Process was facing serious challenges, prompting me to write to my parish priest in Cabinteely with a suggestion that we, in the churches in the south, had a part to play in promoting dialogue between the

churches in Northern Ireland. Our parish had a long
tradition of dialogue with our neighbouring Church of
Ireland parish. Due to this association I was well ac-
quainted with the Rector, Rev Ferran Glenfield. Some
weeks later I got a call from Ferran, asking if we could
we meet, along with Colin Murphy.

We duly met and agreed to set in train a move to
bring parishioners together for a weekend of prayer and
dialogue. Naturally there was only one place where
such a dialogue could take place — Glencree. Our meeting was blessed with glorious Glencree winter weather
— cold and a heavy snowfall — reminding me of the
conditions that those German refugee children had had
to endure.

Further meetings in Newcastle, County Down and in
Glencree strengthened the bonds of friendship and
forged even stronger bonds between those of us from
Kill o' the Grange and Cabinteely who have participated
in the Churches Programme. It has flourished, with a
constant core group but with many others, noticeably
many younger people, now involved, thus giving us the
encouragement to keep our thoughts and actions focused on the prize – a change of hearts and minds that
will see Northern Ireland at peace.

The Glencree Churches Programme has constantly
challenged participants; it has brought into sharp focus
the importance of recognising that insensitive words
used to reinforce one's own thoughts (never prejudices!)
can have far-reaching consequences. It has been a source
of great learning to see how people from diverse and
bitterly opposed traditions who have had to cope with
awful personal tragedies have been able to deal with

such experiences. I have listened, sometimes in awe, to people whose personal experiences seem to come from the pages of some horror story. I have listened to their stories, sometimes with difficulty — for fear that I might cry for them, when they are long done with crying. What use would my tears be in such a situation?

In trying to do justice to the range of challenges that the Glencree Churches' Programme has posed for participants, it would be foolish to focus too closely on single elements. To isolate one instant at one meeting as being a defining moment or interpret one meeting's conclusions as being more important than another or to highlight comments by one individual as having been the inspiration for major progress would be to miss the value of these encounters.

Many of the protagonists of the past 35 years of the Troubles have had exposure to the ethos of Glencree. They have been given the opportunity to open up to others of different traditions in ways that would not be otherwise possible, they have been challenged, they have come and gone quietly and are the better for it. They can never claim that their experience of Glencree threatened their place or standing on this island. They cannot ignore that which is irrefutable — that is, simply, that peace and reconciliation start from within.

One of the highlights of the work of Glencree was the visit of The Prince of Wales in February 2002. Acknowledgements by the Irish and British governments that the work of the Glencree Centre for Peace and Reconciliation is, and remains, a vital ingredient in the ongoing quest for peace and reconciliation in these islands were timely and well-deserved. The fulsome words of apology by The Prince of Wales did not fall on deaf ears. Their meaning and intent were quite clear and it remains for those who have been wedded to violence for so long to see how important it is they now make the essential leaps of faith that the search for peace demands.

Central to all that has happened in these past few years has been the ethos of Glencree, a Glencree I have come to know and respect in so many ways. One can sometimes feel disheartened on seeing the youth of our cities being depicted as drunken, violent people without a care for themselves or others. Then one comes face to face with volunteers from overseas and from Ireland who give their time for free in support of the work of the Glencree Centre.

I hope that Glencree will continue to be a place for peace, ready to give comfort, support and encouragement to all who go there.

Marcus Hopkins

Marcus Hopkins has been working with Glencree since the end of 2002. His interests include the sociology and philosophy of religions, education and Irish–British relations at street level. He is currently doing a PhD with the Institute of Education at Manchester Metropolitan University. Born in England to a Northern Irish mother and a Catholic English father, he has lived on this island for over ten years and has been a regular visitor for nearly 40.

Glencree: A deeper form of learning

DESPITE IT BEING A NON-RELIGIOUS organisation, it is the spiritual dimension of Glencree that has influenced me the most. Even though Glencree is not a Christian organisation, its ideology seems to me to mirror the revolutionary ethos of Christ: befriending those who are regarded as your enemies as well as showing real compassion for innocent victims.

It is a place where unexpected things have happened and where at times the expected has not. Like the evening when the participants of the Churches Programme decided to retire early, a very rare event, and where instead, I ended up in the company of a group completely unknown to me, where an accidental conversation lasted many many hours, and will never be forgotten: a real insight into what I had perceived to be true for several

years, but until then had never really known. And I
don't even think that Glencree knew who was there that
night — one of the many unknown people "involved" in
Irish politics on this island as well as in Britain.

Perhaps what will never be known are the emotional
and dynamic outputs of Glencree: the ways in which the
organisation has acted as a catalyst for so many to engage
in their own attempts at building a peace, or at least some
kind of peace. Using the most simplistic of peace-building
processes — those of listening and talking — Glencree
and its participants have somehow altered mindsets,
sometimes in a very minor but important way, at other
times far more profoundly for the individual concerned.
It is the simplicity of the process that helps to break down
myth and misunderstanding. It is the simplicity that has
encouraged others to replicate the idea in their own lives,
in their own communities and even overseas.

Perhaps the major successes of Glencree will never
be known. In fact, no perhaps about it: many of Glencree's achievements will never be publicly known:
achievements that are spoken of in Leitrim and Kildare,
in Fermanagh and Wales, in Manchester and Spain, and
who knows where else.

Participants at Glencree have taught me the essen-
tiality of engaging with others: all others, irrespective of
who they are now, and who they once were. Learning
from the families of those killed is such a deep and
meaningful form of education, as is learning from those
who have killed. An education that is so intense, so
meaningful and emotional, so indelible.

Obviously there are times when Glencree gets it
wrong. But, if Glencree were faultless, then it wouldn't

be doing what it does best, which is taking a gamble on ideas and people that others simply leave alone. And I'm truly happy to be able to say that in my short time at Glencree, things have gone wrong, mistakes have been made: happy because mistakes are one of the most fundamental forms of learning for us all. If it wasn't for people being brave enough to try, despite all the odds being against them, then who in the world would be brave enough to be entrepreneurs, who would risk aiding the Samaritan, who would defend the unfashionable causes, who would support the minorities. So here's wishing Glencree a future full of mistaken ideas, and because of them, a future full of successes. The day Glencree becomes perfect is the day the heart of the organisation dies.

Another form of learning that has come from working with Glencree has been knowledge of the huge amount of peace-building work that goes on unannounced in local communities everywhere. The unsung heroes who do so much for so little in return, from priests and ministers to former combatants of all shades and, perhaps the most important of all, the families of those who were killed. And it's because of Glencree that I'll never forget that, for so many, the conflict can never end. Emotional turmoil will hopefully lessen, but it will always be there, a point to remember when people talk loosely of the "post-conflict" situation. Because of Glencree's participants, I shall never forget the horror of their reality.

It would be impossible for me to talk about Glencree without mentioning the learning I get from the volunteers: whether they come from Ireland, north or south, or from further afield, whether from other EU States, Africa or America, or anywhere else on the globe — people who give up so much time to do so much, often doing the work that nobody sees, but that is essential to all.

Working with Glencree has increased my personal perception of there being a lack of interest in Northern Ireland from many people in Britain, and from many in the south. Just how anyone can lack interest in the suffering that has gone on for so long on our doorsteps is almost beyond me. How did those of us from either the island of Britain or the Republic of Ireland allow so much suffering to go on in the North for so long? This is a question the people of Northern Ireland have a right to have answered. And Glencree allows that sort of question to be asked. No need to be nice, just honest.

Glencree seems to bring out the philosophical and the spiritual in me. The failures have been the successes. Hard to explain, I know, but Glencree is spiritual and philosophical to me in so many ways. So the successes are known to those who know, and there's no need to tell the world. Indeed, the world can never know because to tell would be to break so many confidences. And Glencree is all about creating those confidences through trust and understanding.

Finally, participants at Glencree have taught me the importance of remembering all of those who have suffered so badly that they can never forget. Through their stories told at Glencree and through their bravery at engaging in dialogue with others, I promise them that neither will I.

Liz Iwaskiw

Liz Iwaskiw is the sole proprietor of a conflict management firm (Iwaskiw & Associates) in Lethbridge, Alberta, Canada. She has a certificate in Conflict Management and a Bachelor's degree in Political Science and Psychology. She was awarded Chartered Mediator status in 2001 from the ADR Institute of Canada. Iwaskiw & Associates offers a full range of conflict management services with a particular emphasis on the mediation of workplace disputes and the creation and delivery of conflict management training to corporations, governments and non-profit organisations in Canada and abroad.

I FIRST CAME TO GLENCREE in 1997 and found myself enchanted not just by the beauty and serenity of the setting but more so by the determined sense of purpose I felt from the staff and volunteers. These were people on a mission and their enthusiasm was infectious. Over the course of the last seven years I have taught at Glencree 17 times to politicians, community leaders, paramilitaries, Travellers, women's groups, victims groups, kids and the Glencree family. The courses themselves were satisfying (which I will get to later) but what surprises me still is the buzz I get from just helping, whether it be washing dishes or painting the window sills of derelict buildings (now long gone) or hanging curtains in bedrooms or hoovering the Canada room in the wee hours of the morning after a good "session" with my students.

How could these menial tasks afford such contentment? It's what I call the Magic of Glencree.

Numerous scholars over the years have suggested that man's highest calling is to have purpose, a sense that what one is doing is worthwhile, and Glencree is the most "purpose-full" place I have ever been. To be in the company of volunteers from war-torn countries such as Bosnia, Serbia, Nepal, Burma and the Congo (to name but a few), it is an honour and a privilege to wash floors with them as they share their stories. They have taught me more about conflict than any course I have taken in Canada! To plant flowers and sweep the pathways in preparation for a state visit in the hopes that some further funding may be forthcoming to allow Glencree programmes to continue; what work have I done that is more important than that? In this crazy world today where so many prostitute themselves for profit, Glencree is a place where people are working very hard for very little simply because it is the right thing to do and I consider myself blessed to have been a tiny part of that.

Each time I come to Glencree it is to teach courses in conflict management. My focus is to help people stop trying to change the "other guy" and work on themselves and their own behaviour instead. No matter how hard we try to make other people change we cannot make them do, or say, or think, anything other than they choose. I help participants recognise the futility of that approach and empower them to take responsibility for themselves. I teach them to engage rather than confront, to understand rather than convince and that the conversation itself is their goal regardless of whatever solutions either party may have in mind. These are the principles I teach and I know them to be effective from the feedback I get from participants.

But I have a guilty confession to make. No matter who the participants are, I learn as much from them as they do from me. In each and every course someone enlightens me in some way that makes the next course better. Educated people can become arrogant but the people I meet at Glencree have so far helped me avoid that trap. The black-and-white issues I have in my head when I arrive are invariably turned grey around the edges, forcing me to rethink. The exercises and examples I use have become more culture-specific as participants provide me with a reality check from the perspective of those who live in conflict. They are the experts, not I! My ability to convey the course material, both there and here at home, has been immeasurably improved by their input.

I have taught courses in Belfast and Londonderry as well as Glencree and I must confess a preference for the Glencree setting. When I first came to Glencree and heard of their philosophy of getting people "away from the troubles", I admit I thought they were being self-serving. Over the years, however, I have come to appreciate the value of bringing people to the Wicklow Mountains, not only for the calm and peaceful setting but also for the camaraderie that result from being together for the entire course.

Most people who teach workshops recognise that some of the most valuable interaction happens outside the classroom. I can tell you that many valuable exchanges have taken place over breakfast or lunch or dinner or over a pint in the evening. Even more important than that, however, is the point Glencree made back when I started which I did not appreciate at the time – that people living in conflict areas have to get out of that area to think straight! Teaching in Londonderry or Belfast is so much more difficult because the conflict is right outside the window. I have had participants, who took a course in Belfast or Londonderry, come to Glencree at a later date for the same course and tell me it made so much more sense to them this time. Of course, part of that could be due to repetition but I can tell you their very demeanour in the classroom is different. They are more relaxed, more receptive and far more engaged, I believe, because they feel safe.

How do I close my "Ode to Glencree"? By telling you that I am a better person for having been there? Absolutely! That I am a better mediator and trainer as a result of my experiences there? Without a doubt! That I will come back each and every time I am asked, whether it be to teach conflict management or clean toilets? You bet!

Happy 30th Birthday Glencree Centre for Reconciliation!

Margaret Joyce

Margaret Joyce is an experienced Organisation Consultant, Executive Coach and Trainer who works from holistic and humanistic perspectives. Her background is in Human Resources Management and Organisation Development both for large multi-national businesses and public sector services. Contemporaneous with her business career, for the last fifteen years Margaret has undertaken training in Gestalt, Psychodynamic, Systemic and Shamanic approaches which she uses to inform her work with individuals, groups and organisations. Margaret is committed to her own on-going personal development which supports her to work in integrity, compassion and wisdom. Margaret was born in north Tipperary, and has lived for many years in London.

The Women's Programme

BEING INVITED TO WRITE THIS HAS given me the opportunity to reflect on the Women's Programme at Glencree as it is today and what it is that we are working towards. This piece is written to provide a sense of what we do and how we work together.

I got involved in the Women's Programme a few years ago through offering my consulting services as a gift to Glencree because I believe passionately in peaceful process. As someone who lives outside Ireland, I wanted to stay connected with my Irishness and my roots in a way that delighted me and gave something back also. At the time, the Women's Programme had gone through the first stages of its evolution, in part beginning to discover what it was not or did not want to become as well as some of what it intended to be. At that stage, the programme was mainly run as a series of one-off workshops.

The intention of the Women's Programme is to engage women from all sides and aspects of life in Ireland in a process of peaceful dialogue, growth and development. This group has now expanded to include women from many different backgrounds and increasingly we are becoming a fairly good representation of all the women of Ireland.

The Women's Programme has evolved to include several aspects: it is a space for peaceful dialogue and discussion; it provides a training and development programme designed to underpin peacemaking; it is a supportive network for women to share, learn together and support each other in our personal and professional development. I have detailed below a little about each of these aspects of the current programme to give a sense of what it is that we do and hopefully also some sense of the extraordinary, creative, demanding and exciting ways in which we work together in those activities.

We co-create a safe space for peaceful dialogue and discussion where current and emergent issues of any nature, from the personal to the political, can be engaged with. We are discovering that the separation between those two can often be very small, if it exists at all, and we all come to this with our interestingly different identities. In itself, this provides challenge to our openness to others and our honesty with ourselves. In learning how to dialogue with each other in a safe space with respect, honesty, care and integrity, we can better take those skills we learn through that experience back to our "real lives" and integrate this into the places where we work, where we live, to our communities, with our neighbours and to our schools.

It offers a training and development programme in some of what we regard as the basic building blocks of peaceful community. This is an incremental programme of learning that aims to give individuals the skills to understand their own personal process of change, learning and development; and to train them to be able to take those skills back to their respective communities and share them there. The programme currently includes work on self-esteem and self-image, communication and assertiveness skills, principled negotiation and conflict resolution, group process and development, valuing difference and managing diversity. At present the programme provides a Certificate of Participation from Glencree and it is our intention to achieve formal external accreditation during the next year. This programme has run for a foundation year and will continue to develop further subjects and levels to meet the needs of those participating.

The Women's Programme is becoming a support network for our shared learning at personal and professional levels. Members of the main programme meet in small geographically based Peer Learning Sets between large group workshops in order to practise skills, prepare for the next group workshop and discuss how their projects are developing. We use this process to consolidate our learning and to provide a strong and valuable support network, particularly when those in the group take this work back into their respective communities. Underlining these groups' experiences, members learn about group dynamics, process and development, which are valuable transferable skills required in all well-functioning communities and societies.

I will give a taste of how we work together now. These workshops and learning events are filled at different times with stretch, laughter, insights, tears and fears. Through this we learn to bring more of ourselves to the process, extending our self-acceptance and through that, our ability to accept others too. The combination of experience that the participants bring to the group and the depth of work that people are willing to engage in is inspiring. Like any well-functioning group, there is space for celebration and times when shadow and more challenging feelings emerge. Along with all the deep stuff, there are also social learning times and just social time when we go out for a short rest or have a drink and a chat and enjoy the craic.

For the future, as a group we discuss where we could take this work and, like any healthy group, several ideas, opinions and potential directions emerge. As well as expanding how and where we take this back into our respective communities, there are a number of other possibilities. These could include engaging with other women from equally "troubled" nations, in particular where there has been a sibling type issue and/or it may be useful to consider how we develop and support more women to engage in the electoral political process so that women's energies and contributions are better utilised. Indeed, to better understand what the qualitative difference we can make as women will be an exciting learning experience in itself. True to the spirit of the group and Glencree itself, our future direction continues to engage us while we are getting on with the current work.

The Women's Programme is always open and actively interested in hearing from or engaging with individuals or other women's groups so that we may continue to extend ourselves to be all we can be and to make our valuable contribution to peace-making.

Isobel Kane

*Isobel Kane was born in Campsie, Eglinton, County London-
derry but spent her childhood in Hillsborough, County Down,
until she moved in 1968 to London. She returned to Lisburn
in 1973 where she worked with the Southern Health Board as
Area Domestic Services Manager. In 1987 she moved to Manchester and lectured in Accommodation Management and
Tourism at Manchester Metropolitan University before returning to Ireland to live in Dublin in 1994. Isobel is married
to Alfie and they have two grown-up daughters.*

H AVING MOVED TO DUBLIN in 1994, and not working
outside the home for the first time in 25 years, I
welcomed a telephone call from an "old friend" inviting
me to a Peace Centre he was involved in — the Glencree
Centre for Reconciliation.

On arrival at the centre I was enraptured by the
tranquillity of the site, with the buildings nestling in the
Wicklow Hills and the Sugar Loaf Mountain visible
from practically every window. The "spirit" of Glencree
was so apparent and the enthusiasm of the staff — in
particular Ian White the Director — helped me decide to
involve myself voluntarily in supporting the work of
Glencree and the staff. The task assigned to me was to
ensure that there were minimum standards set and
achieved within this residential centre (this included the
catering, housekeeping and laundry activities, etc.).

To assist me with this task, in particular the kitchen area, I involved a long-standing college friend, Geraldine McAleese. She commenced as catering manager and did a super job training the volunteers of the time, producing meals, introducing the necessary catering, health and safety procedures. Geraldine still works at Glencree as housekeeping manager.

Drawing up the necessary standards was not a difficult task for me but the raising of the necessary funds to upgrade the accommodation and purchase of equipment was a bit more time-consuming. To this end I formed a development committee and together we organised fund-raising events, e.g. sponsored walks in Powerscourt Estate, bridge mornings at the centre and asking the business community to assist in whatever way they could. Some of the early donations included carpet tiles, laundry equipment, beds, mattresses and pictures. All donations where most gratefully accepted and helped make the accommodation more comfortable and homely.

In 1995 John Finnerty produced a corporate video for Glencree called "Let's Get Together", which was sponsored by Alfie Kane at Eircom plc. The video explained the work carried out at Glencree and allowed participants to tell their stories as to why they had come to the Centre and what they felt they had achieved from the programmes there. This video was most useful when Ian White, accompanied on occasions by myself, gave presentations on the work of Glencree with the intentions of obtaining sponsorship from the business community. In 1999, the Glencree Business Club was formed and today 29 companies are members. These corporates support us financially or donate goods in kind. Without them, it

would be impossible to finance many of our programmes. One of the advantages in supporting Glencree
is that sponsors are able to use our facilities for "away
days", staff training, board meetings, etc.

The main programme work when I joined involved
schools, young people and politicians from all over these
islands. We wanted to develop Glencree as a "safe
place" for many of the people involved in the peace-
building work in Northern Ireland and elsewhere. Such
was the nature of the work that we were unable to give
it media attention, a fact that makes fund-raising all the
more demanding and difficult.

After upgrading the kitchen and residential accommodation in the main building, our next task was to ex-
pand the residential and conference facilities in order to
facilitate the increasing demand for programme activity.
We concentrated our energies on completing the Wicklow Wing, named after Eleanor, Lady Wicklow, a founder member of Glencree. This was funded by the International Fund for Ireland and we were very honoured to
have Dr. Mo Mowlam MP, Secretary of State for Northern Ireland, unveil the plaque at the opening of this
building in 1998.

As a member of the International Women's Club of
Dublin I was privileged to meet women from 45 countries whose husbands were working in the diplomatic
service or in the Irish corporate sector. As a result of
contacts I established in the club, many of these people
have furnished bedrooms in the style of their homeland
and had them named after their countries. This unique
programme has resulted in residential participants being
now allocated to a room that is identified by the name of

a country rather than simply by a number. This has not only been financially very successful but is very pleasing for the occupants of the rooms.

With the signing of the Good Friday Agreement in 1998, the demand for our work began to increase and Glencree became a very well-known peace centre. In the 10 years that I have been involved with Glencree I have seen the numbers attending our programmes increase from 2,000 to 7,000 per annum.

We no longer had to maintain confidentiality to the same extent as we had initially. The commencement of other programmes such as LIVE (Let's Involve the Victims' Experience), Ex-combatants' and Churches' programmes meant that further residential and administrative space was required. Thanks to contacts established by Alfie Kane and Ian White, the Office of Public Works agreed to renovate the original barracks building, now called The Bridge. This was opened in early 2002 by Brian Cowen, Minister for Foreign Affairs and HRH The Prince of Wales. The Bridge is now fully furnished and operational. It has ten bedrooms that have been furnished by embassies: (England, Wales, Scotland, Northern Ireland, South Africa, Australia, etc.) There are also two conference rooms, a boardroom (sponsored by Superquinn Ltd.), a coffee shop, exhibition space and a peace resource centre (sponsored by Ulster Bank).

Our next project is the upgrading of the offices in the original building and the renovation of the old armoury. The Office of Public Works will carry out this renovation work in 2004 and we will re-locate the coffee shop to the armoury facility, thereby freeing up more exhibition space in The Bridge.

I have thoroughly enjoyed being involved not only in the development of the site but also in the peace-building work that is carried out at the centre. I have been a member of the Council of Glencree since 1995 and have been a member of the Glencree Executive for the last two years. This has been a super way of being completely involved with the staff, the work of the centre and the development of both buildings and programmes. I look forward to many more years of involvement.

John Kelly

John Kelly was born in Ballyjamesduff, County Cavan. John joined Working for Peace in 1973 and Glencree in 1974 and served as Treasurer in the mid 1970s during constant financial crises! He participated in many weekend work camps digging the same trench innumerable times in bad weather but excellent company.

A Tale of Two Cities

IN THE LATE SIXTIES I ATTENDED University in Dublin and remember vividly the student revolution, which had spread across the university campuses from Nantes in France. It was a remarkable time of protest with much discussion on political and bureaucratic issues, fired by the success of the Civil Rights Movement in the United States. Housing was one of the issues in Ireland, both north and south, and the Dublin Housing Action Committee had led street protests and there were similar protests in Derry and Belfast.

In late 1969 I went to work in Belfast for a period of three years until the winter of 1972. It was a time of serious social and political ferment there and the paramilitary organisations were increasingly active. I lived in Belfast Monday to Friday and spent the weekends in Dublin. As the destabilisation in Northern Ireland took hold those weeks in Belfast and weekends in Dublin highlighted for me the huge gulf that the short 100 miles between the two cities represented. The differences in politics and creed were so wide both within Northern Ireland and between north and south.

During those years in the early seventies I met many people from a wide spectrum of opinion in Northern Ireland, visited Loyalist and Republican Clubs and attended services in churches of most denominations. I went to Ian Paisley's Free Presbyterian Church in Ravenhill Road, much to the amusement of my Loyalist workmates who had christened me "Red Socks" — Ian's name for the Pope at the time!

I witnessed so much unfair pain in Belfast. I can still see the frightened children, screaming pregnant women and tearful old men. The office I worked in was bombed by accident and many of my colleagues injured. I was in another office at the time on the toss of a coin. I felt my denominational Christianity background and my sense of political nationality were proving quite inadequate for what was happening.

Working for Peace

One Friday in July 1972, a particularly horrific series of bombings took place, killing many in Belfast and as I drove to Dublin I felt more helpless than usual. A number of people in Dublin, reflecting desperation with what was happening, decided to hold a protest vigil and a sponsored walk. I joined this protest and found that at least walking in open protest and saying a few prayers seemed better than cursing the darkness. A public statement was issued that the protest was against all acts of violence —

no matter from what quarter — and also that those who abhorred violence had to accept the logic of demands for social and economic justice. After that, a small *ad hoc* committee met to reflect on the meaning of peace, of violence and non-violence and to discuss what activities a peace group might undertake. Then in October the *ad hoc* committee called a meeting to which those participants in the protest vigil and walk were invited. Some of those who attended had been involved in arranging rest periods in Dublin for a group of young Belfast mothers and their children and in organising weekend visits of Belfast teenagers to the homes of Dublin families with teenagers from different backgrounds and traditions.

The people at this first meeting decided to stay together as a group to try to combat violence and promote non-violent means of achieving social and political justice. The next step was to start a Church Action Group, which visited clergy of various Churches to encourage interdenominational activity. St Andrews Parish, Westland Row, agreed to invite the clergy of the other five Christian churches in the area to hold an Ecumenical Bible Service for Peace and this took place on 13 December 1972 with 1,400 people attending. A Political Action Group was also formed to visit public representatives, encouraging them to speak out for non-violence. In ways these were naïve simplistic endeavours but you felt it was a way of expressing some response to the failures that were resulting in many innocent deaths.

At a weekend seminar/teach-in of the group in early December, the name "Working for Peace" was adopted and the idea of a residential centre for rest, reconciliation and peace education was put forward.

Glencree Conception

In early 1973, Working for Peace called a press conference at which the aims of the group were described. A public meeting themed "Peace and the People" was held followed by a series of well-attended meetings that spring.

In February it was also decided that Working for Peace should look into the possibility of setting up a reconciliation centre somewhere in Ireland. During the summer of 1973 a company in Newbridge, County Kildare put a hostel at the group's disposal and groups, both Catholic and Protestant, from conflict areas in Northern Ireland were given short breaks there. The experience gained by the group, together with the example, encouragement and advice from The Corrymeela Community in Northern Ireland, convinced the Working for Peace group more than ever of the possibilities for reconciliation work that a permanent centre would afford. Soon afterwards, the old reformatory in Glencree was identified and by spring of 1974 the Glencree Centre for Reconciliation had been legally established and given a temporary lease on much of the complex by the Board of Works.

In March 1974 Working for Peace organised the first Peace Week with the theme "Respect". A number of organisations joined in the Peace Week endeavour, including the Irish Commission for Justice and Peace, Pax Christi, Peace Point, Society of Friends Peace Group, Voluntary Services International, Women's Voluntary Emergency Service, Ballyfermot Peace Corps and many of these supported the Glencree project.

During Peace Week 1974 a new television documentary entitled *The Steel Shutter* was shown in the International Film Theatre in Earlsfort Terrace, Dublin. The film captured the spectrum of people's attitudes in Northern Ireland by filming a roundtable discussion among "on the ground" people from different backgrounds and traditions. The film illustrated the idea of a neutral forum where views could be expressed in a caring, nonjudgemental environment and constituted, I believe, an important pathfind in the reconciliation journey that was to continue in Glencree.

The first volunteer workcamp began at the Centre on 12 July 1974, an auspicious day. The work had just begun!

André Lascaris

Dr André Lascaris is a Dutch Dominican. He received his PhD at Oxford University and lectured in Pretoria, Amsterdam and Nijmegen. He was editor of a theological weekly, fulfilled several administrative functions in his Order, and was involved in peace work for Northern Ireland from 1973 until 1992. He has published numerous articles and books on conflict, violence, forgiveness and reconciliation. He has been a member of the staff of the Dominican Study Centre for Theology and Society at Nijmegen, the Netherlands, since its foundation in 1988.

May Glencree soon be able to close its doors

IN 1973, ONE YEAR BEFORE GLENCREE opened its doors, I was invited to become a member of staff of a conference for influential Northern Irishmen in a quiet and spiritual atmosphere in the Netherlands. The director of Dutch adult education centre "De Half", the late At van Rhine, a Presbyterian minister, asked me to participate in the conference because he wanted a Catholic priest to make the Roman Catholic Northern Irish people feel represented on the staff. The Irish Council of Churches became our Northern Irish counterpart. After more conferences had taken place, a trust was formed in 1975: the Dutch Northern Irish Advisory Committee, its constitution stipulating that no conference could be undertaken without the consent of the Northern Irish members. In 1992 the committee was dissolved; it had run its course. In September 1973 our first conference was held — one of the participants was a Mr Colin Murphy. From participants at the first conference a new request for a conference was made and after this one even more conferences were organised, altogether 18 between 1973 and 1983. In the late 1970s, the security situation in Northern Ireland improved. The necessity of travelling to the Netherlands to meet people became less evident. Because our work remained in demand, we organised weekends in Northern Ireland itself from 1981 onwards, mainly in Corrymeela, the ecumenical adult education centre near Ballycastle.

Our work was carried out on the basis of the tradition of Dutch adult education. The starting point of this kind of work is the conviction that every adult is responsible for their learning process. The facilitator initiates this process, guards it and tries to shape it. The goal of this learning process is to enable a person to make a contribution to social change and to the improvement of the situation in which they find themselves. The person is part of this process. The learning process takes place in a group. This group represents to a certain extent the social and personal situations in which the participants are living. It is composed of people who share an issue, a subject or theme that to some extent unites them, and some awareness of what they want to learn. Though some input from outside the group may be necessary, the group itself is often quite knowledgeable. The greater part of any conference is used to communicate to one another the knowledge that is contained in the group itself. The facilitator uses different methods to bring this knowledge to the surface and to promote the exchange of facts, emotions and experience. Every participant shares responsibility for what happens in the group. He should feel free and secure: "everything said in this room remains in this room". The place where these exchanges take place must provide a hospitable environment. At such conferences, the informal part — meeting one another as persons and individuals — is at least as important as the official programme.

In 1981 our committee had its first contacts with Glencree via Colin Murphy. In the spring of 1982, we met Geoffrey Corry and some of his colleagues. It was clear at that time that Glencree was running into difficulties, financially and otherwise. The late Roel Kaptein worked twice with staff and volunteers to uncover together the goals Glencree could eventually set for itself. A bible weekend followed in May 1985. I personally did a staff training in 1987. In 1988 our committee was informed that Glencree had to close down, but at the same time a period of reflection started. In this period I had occasional meetings with several people involved in Glencree. For me a very remarkable meeting took place with Una O'Higgins O'Malley in her home to discuss the draft of a mission statement for Glencree. It was a privilege to meet her. I am not sure how much of our discussion, if any, survived in the present mission statement [*Editors' note: 95 per cent of it did!*]. Glencree opened its doors again in 1994. In the succeeding year I gave a brief lecture, took part in a forum, and was present once or twice at events on a Sunday afternoon. So, my contribution to the life of Glencree was altogether modest.

Glencree has chosen to be a secular centre. In the context of Ireland this seems to me a good choice. Its theme, "Ireland and its neighbours", offers sufficient inspiration to organise a great variety of conferences. Still, I am slightly worried about the future. Unfortunately, the more peace there will be, the less money will be available. In fact, when a political agreement has been made, the true peace is still far away. A political peace gives some breathing space. This has to be used to achieve reconciliation of some kind so that violence will not erupt again. However, most people tend to think that peace has been achieved and that it is a waste to spend money and time on "places for peace". People may lose interest, avoid "wasting" their time by attending conferences and spending some of their money on a place like Glencree. Another worry is that Glencree is not as yet very accessible and that its accommodation is austere. It would be a great pity if Glencree had to close down again because of those reasons.

There is only one good reason for Glencree to close down: to have achieved fully which it has been founded for — an Ireland in true peace, where people do not rival with one another any more, do not scapegoat, do not accuse; a world, thus, in peace. I hope that Glencree will soon be able to close down because this goal has been achieved. For the time being, I hope that may people will continue giving their talents, time and money to Glencree so that it can go on to inspire, challenge and encourage people on their common way to peace.

James Edward Hazlett Lynch

*Dr James Edward Hazlett Lynch was born outside Donemana
in County Tyrone, Northern Ireland, and lived and was edu-
cated for some 20 years within five miles of the west Tyrone/
Londonderry border with the Irish Republic. He later lived and
worked on the south Armagh border for almost nine years. He
was ordained into the Christian Ministry in 1979, trained as a
teacher and then as a counsellor. He is currently the project co-
ordinator/director of victims' group, West Tyrone Voice.*

M Y WORK IS IN A SUPPORT CAPACITY for those who
have been bereaved, injured or traumatised by
terrorists during the 35 years of sectarianism and ethnic
cleansing of the Pro-British community (Protestant and
Catholic) in Northern Ireland. The work is emotionally
demanding, and we do it because it is essential in promoting the recovery of victims, which in itself is essential if we are to establish reconciliation in this land.

I got involved with Glencree about four years ago.
Initially, I was hesitant because I was concerned that the
all-inclusive orientation of Glencree would entail meeting with murderers, and this was just too much, and
could be dangerous.

The LIVE programme offers victims from the United
Kingdom and the Irish Republic the opportunity to meet
and share their experiences of terrorist violence, how it
has impacted on them, what it has cost them, and how

they have coped, or not coped, as a result. Glencree has facilitated these meetings, giving victims the opportunity to display their non-sectarian credentials. Protestant and Catholic victims have no real difficulty in supporting each other. Murder is murder regardless of the cause or creed.

It was also great to hear terrorist victims from Great Britain saying that if it were not for people like us, they would not come to Glencree. They feel we have an experiential understanding of what it is like to have loved ones and close personal friends violently murdered or severely maimed and traumatised by the terrorists who have acted outside the law, without justification, and have done so with impunity.

While we had hoped that it would have been useful to meet with terrorists and confront them with what they have done, the opposite has been our experience. They either do not turn up for sessions, or, when they do, they will not give us answers to our questions. They try to tell us who we are, or who we should be, they give us lectures on their mythological version of history (British and Irish), but no answers as to why they have murdered our loved ones, and maimed our relatives and friends. Nor will they tell us "the war is over"; therefore we can only conclude it is still on!

The use of disinfected language (*ex-combatants* instead of *terrorists*) is an unfortunate attempt by Glencree to make terrorist killers out to be better than they really are, and equates them with the legitimate forces of law and order (north and south of the border). This has given the impression that Glencree staff believe that what the terrorists did was legitimate and defensible, something we simply cannot understand. This leaves victims frustrated, angry, disillusioned, and asking why on earth they are involved with an organisation like Glencree at all? Some people even believe that Glencree exists to salve the consciences of the terrorists.

The insensitivity of Glencree to the feelings of victims leaves much to be desired, as demonstrated in the stay of convicted terrorist, Dessie O'Hare (aka the "Border Fox") at the Centre. To defend this by saying that they were asked to have him by the Republic's government, or one of its agencies, was no excuse.

The partnership between Glencree and the governments of the United Kingdom and Republic of Ireland is too close for it to be helpful to victims, or even trusted by them. Victims ask me, "To what extent is Glencree simply promoting government policy, given that it has embraced the inclusivist definition of victim?" Is Glencree the "eyes and ears" of the respective governments? For victims and terrorist perpetrators to be *lumped together* by a mis-definition of victim is to re-victimise the victims. Yet, who cares?

This is disappointing to victims and to those who care for them. I suppose it comes down to the fact that only a *real victim* truly understands what it is like to have a loved one targeted for death by psychopathic killers who now masquerade as political statesmen and peacemakers.

The role played by some sections of the Roman Catholic Church in IRA terrorism is also a cause of concern for victims. There are at least eight Roman Catholic priests known to us as having been actively involved in terrorist activities. Their bishops were also "in the know" about these activities, and relocated the priests elsewhere when this became evident. The church also accorded the full rights of their religion to IRA volunteers who were killed on active duty, either by the security forces or by their own bombs, etc. It was at Glencree that I learned from a Roman Catholic friend that within his church in Northern Ireland, a deceased parishioner could hardly get even a curate to perform the funeral service, while at IRA funerals, clergy were "tripping over each other to be seen at the funeral".

This does nothing to help people trust their Roman Catholic neighbours. Surely Glencree ought to be encouraging the Roman Catholic Church to apologise for the hurt it has caused. If this apology is not forthcoming, some will see the church as the religious wing of IRA/Sinn Féin, and that would be another barrier to reconciliation.

On the reconciliation issue, the notion is conveyed that it is the victims who have to be reconciled to the terrorists, and this has caused immense hurt to victims. In the Judeo-Christian tradition, it is always the *offended* party who calls for the *offenders* to be reconciled to it, never the other way round. This is what victims have been doing through their involvement in Glencree. Of all people in Northern Ireland, it is the *victims* who want peace and reconciliation, for they are the people who have suffered most during the genocidal years of terrorist violence. The "peace and reconciliation industry" is actually re-crucifying victims when it implies and even suggests that the offended (that is, the victims) must be reconciled to the offenders (that is, the perpetrators).

Further, reconciliation is an act of sheer grace shown by the *offended* party to the *offender*. Victims have shown amazing mercy to those whose purpose in life was to

murder them, by not retaliating. They have also taken
risks for peace, and have met with perpetrators, but
what did they get in return? Nothing — not even an
apology. The offended party looked for some positive
response from the offenders — like saying "I am sorry",
"it was a mistake to do what I did", "it was wrong" —
but none was forthcoming. In order to hide their barba-
rous deeds, they refuse to describe themselves as terrorists, but as ex-combatants, claiming to be the only legitimate army in Ireland, thus placing themselves *above*
the legitimate forces of law and order in Northern Ireland and the Republic of Ireland. These terms were
adopted to conceal the fact that they *acted outside the law*.
So long as the offenders retain the right and the means
to murder and maim their targets, their commitment to
peace is absent. By their activities, they have created distrust and uncertainty, and have undermined any commitment they claim to have to pursuing peace.

This point can be illustrated by two incidents that
occurred at Glencree. One time when I was there, a
member from the pro-British community was so afraid
to return to Northern Ireland by train with known republican terrorists that he asked me to take him to the
train station in order to get an earlier train home. He
told me that if he was on the same train home, he might
not arrive in Belfast alive.

The other case occurred during a conference which
had amongst its participants people linked with both
republican and loyalist terrorists. The unreality of any
progress towards reconciliation was seen in the fact that
the loyalists, for their own safety, had barricaded themselves in their bedroom for fear that the republicans

might attack them during the night. Reconciliation? Does this speak of progress towards peace? You decide.

It is difficult to see where reconciliation is happening within the "reconciliation industry", and there appears to be little enthusiasm for "forging swords into plough-shares" by the Provisional IRA and their fellow travellers.

Victims of terrorism have reached out a hand to their enemies by not joining paramilitaries and seeking revenge, but, sadly, their gesture has not been reciprocated. This can be seen very clearly in the voting trends in Northern Ireland. One of these trends is a most disappointing aspect of the situation. The pro-British electorate in Northern Ireland has moved decisively away from parties linked with paramilitaries, but unfortunately, the pro-Irish community in the province has moved significantly towards support for parties with fully operational private armies behind them to assist them in their negotiations. The meteoric rise in electoral support for IRA/Sinn Féin has increased distrust, and has had a harmful effect on the confidence of the pro-British community. While some people believe that the massive mandate given to IRA/Sinn Féin in recent elections is an indicator that democracy is working, others see it as having similarities to the mandate that Hitler had to ethnically cleanse the Jews. If this is so, then reconciliation is further away than ever. This reality is having a most negative and damaging effect on the reconciliation process, an effect that must be acknowledged.

For Glencree to be the force for good that it aspires to be, it must take the needs and concerns of victims much more seriously than it has done in the past. If the Centre is attempting to bring terrorists to repentance, well and

good, and we will be with you in this. But if not, then
the future for work with victims is being jeopardised.

My identity is Ulster Scots and my orientation is British, something I wish to retain. I have no intention of
resigning my identity to become an Irish citizen, or to
live in a monolithic and sectarian state. We have paid
too high a price for any of us to give up our national
identity at the end of a gun. As the words of the theme
song of the *On Eagle's Wing* musical puts it:

> They've taken our land
> We were killed at their hands
> They've taken our homes away.
> But while we shall live
> Our spirits shall give
> The strength for the fight to stay.

This articulates well the experience of ethnic cleansing
and the conviction of people in my community, and no
matter who tries to wean us away from this, they will be
resisted. We are still committed to pursuing peace and
reconciliation in Northern Ireland, and we hope our fellow countrymen come to see the futility of trying to force
an arrangement that will not be acceptable to real victims. Coercion and reconciliation are mutually exclusive.
Reconciliation cannot be established by force of arms.

In conclusion, Glencree must find a way of dealing
with terrorists and their victims without giving the impression that these are equally deserving of respect and
understanding. There must be greater transparency as to
what is done in the "ex-combatants" (*your* term, not
mine) programmes. I would ask Glencree to find out why
exactly the terrorists murdered our relatives, and how

they justify such murder to themselves and to the victims, seeing Glencree works with terrorists, and how far the Roman Catholic doctrine of "murder without sin", promulgated in Wexford in 1798, explain their actions.

Paddy Joe McClean

*Paddy Joe McClean, a retired teacher, has been a regular con-
tributor over the years to the political weekends at Glencree. A
former chairperson of the Northern Ireland Civil Rights Association he was one of those detained in the internment swoops
in Northern Ireland in August 1971 and forced to undergo
what was identified by the International Court of Human
Rights at Strasbourg as "cruel and degrading treatment". He
was subsequently interned at Long Kesh. A member of the
now suspended Civic Forum, he was a member of the Police
Authority of Northern Ireland and presently sits on Omagh
District Policing Partnership Board.*

IN MY SCHOOLBOOK MORE THAN 50 years ago there was
a story about a fox. This fox was tortured with fleas.
So flea-bitten was he that he could no longer concentrate
on, or even pursue, the means of his own survival. His
body shrank as the fleas multiplied and fed on his blood.
He became gaunt and pain-ridden. His speed deserted
him and, worse still, his prey eluded him. Death seemed
imminent.

At that crisis point his life took a turn for the better
when a new thought struck him. He went to a mossy
bank, gathered as much moss as he could into his mouth
and headed off to a nearby mountain stream. On reach-
ing the water's edge he turned about and walked slowly
backwards against the current into a deeper pool. As the

waters rose to cover, first his tail and then his upper body, the fleas, for safety's sake, swarmed upwards towards, and eventually over, his head and nose and into the dry moss in his mouth.

When his body and then his head sank beneath the water the fox opened his mouth and let the moss float off downstream. With his tormentors gone in the floating moss, he emerged from the water to shake himself on the bank, "free at last", renewed in body and spirit to face again the challenges of life in the wild. By that one act of "letting go" and ridding himself of his unwanted baggage, he had given himself a new lease of life, free from impediment or distraction, to achieve the potential designed for him in the creation plan of the animal world.

At one of our "political" weekends at Glencree, that story was brought vividly back to mind for me when I went for my usual early morning walk. As I made my way out past the old church and headed towards the German graveyard, a fox disappeared from my view across the glen and over the running stream, much to the alarm of a watching and alert bird life. Was this Glencree fox like the fox in my schoolboy storybook? Was he carrying unwanted baggage too? Was his load as heavy as mine? Was he prepared to let go? Was I? At that point in my life, my load was heavy indeed.

A five-year period of internment without trial; being one of the guinea-pigs in the now famous torture experiment; knowing that job opportunities as a teacher and promotion prospects were almost certainly doomed; with five years' wages lost and pension entitlements diminished; being physically separated from a wife and growing family; watching them suffer through no wrongdoing of theirs or mine; having friends and neighbours murdered in a futile, pointless, sectarian conflict in Northern Ireland had left me with enough internal torment to carry for a lifetime. That morning at Glencree the load was almost too heavy to bear or to allow me enjoy the beauty of the morning sun shining on the Featherbeds or to fully appreciate the new hope that the paramilitary ceasefires now offered.

After 25 violent, wasted years and the needless loss of 3,000 precious lives, the various paramilitary groups in Northern Ireland had finally been brought to recognise the futility of their murderous ways. They declared their campaigns of violence at an end and indicated a willingness, if given the opportunity, to enter the political arena as democrats. As a first step in the process of promoting political inclusiveness, the then Taoiseach, Albert Reynolds, had mooted the idea of a Forum of Peace and Reconciliation in Dublin. I had been appointed one of the Northern representatives of my political party, then Democratic Left, shortly afterwards to merge with Irish Labour. Contributions there would require a clearer head than I had at that moment.

That weekend at Glencree, the collective political focus of our workshops ranged as usual across the whole spectrum of personal and political development from conflict to conciliation, from agreement to accommodation and from co-operation towards contentment in a peaceful future and perhaps, if or when possible, to personal reconciliation. It was the start of a journey. Over the years since then, that journey has proved itself to be a slow, tortuous one but a journey nevertheless involving the shedding of baggage, personal, political and, for paramilitaries, war material. It hasn't finished. Does it ever?

But it is a journey that can only be undertaken with others in an environment of safety and confidentiality with honest intent and a recognition that others are in the process of shedding baggage too. Over the years since then, and before, Glencree has been providing that safe environment, its facilitators the encouragement to explore unfamiliar territory and its volunteers the sustenance to enable participants to pursue meaningful dialogue in comfort. The very setting of the Glencree Centre in the remoteness of the Wicklow mountains, with its history spanning other conflicts in Ireland over the centuries, is in itself inspirational and conducive to the search for peace.

At those weekend seminars, conversations with, and conclusions drawn by, representatives of Governments, political party people and community activists, all, at times, benefiting from the experiences of others in comparable areas of conflict across the globe, have been fed back to decision-makers and have helped produce the conditions so necessary to pursue the achievement of peace with justice on this island solely by democratic political means. Valuable lessons have already been learned along the way.

Despite the use of violence to achieve political ends and despite the accumulation of atrocities over 30 years, violent methods have not been rewarded with any victory. Over that same period, politicians have learned to accept the political realities of our times; namely that until they decide otherwise, the people of Ireland have by referendum endorsed the concept of two states existing side by side on this one island — the principle of consent has been agreed. The fact that Human Rights Commissions have been established in those two states to ensure that fair play in all aspects of life will be enjoyed by every citizen is proof positive that equality of opportunity to achieve their full potential will henceforth be the entitlement of every citizen.

Like the fox in the storybook, we have identified the causes of our torment and life has changed in Northern Ireland. We have taken the moss in our collective mouths and slowly and hesitatingly, at different speeds, we have tested the water in a process of "letting go". As the fox was renewed in body and spirit to face the challenges of the wild, we are now being renewed to face our challenges to create a better future; to "accept the things we cannot yet change and, politically, to change the things we can" so that together we can achieve a fairer society on this island in the years ahead. The work of the Glencree for Reconciliation is by no means over.

Enda McDonagh

*One of Ireland's most celebrated theologians and social writ-
ers/commentators, Enda McDonagh was Professor of Moral
Theology and Canon Law at Maynooth from 1958–1995. He
served as a member of the NUI Senate from 1972–1995 and
was a member of the Higher Education Authority from 1985–
1990. He was previously President of the National Conference
of Priests in Ireland and official chaplain to the former President of Ireland and former United Nations Human Rights
Commissioner, Mrs Mary Robinson. Professor McDonagh
was initially appointed chair of UCC's governing body in
1999 and independent chairperson in 2004. Fr McDonagh is a
priest in the diocese of Tuam.*

Remembering the Future

MY EARLY MEMORIES OF THE Glencree project are
vague. I had been a student-friend of Frank Purcell and appreciated the good work he was doing in the
1970s. I had a long connection with Pax Christi and a
more tenuous one with CND Ireland. Peace and reconciliation were lifelong preoccupations which issued in
heavy engagement with the war in Rhodesia/Zimbabwe
in the decade leading up to independence in 1980–81.
Meantime, I had been very engaged with the Northern
Ireland situation, serving for four years on a commission

on Human Rights with people like David Trimble, Sean Farren and the now Bishop of Oxford, Richard Harries. Meantime, I had been drawn more closely into the work of the Irish Association, the longest-established all-island body working for north–south reconciliation, of which I eventually became President. During these decades, I had the privilege of becoming a close friend of Una O'Higgins O'Malley, a key founder of the Glencree Centre and one of my predecessors as President of the Irish Association. Mainly through her influence I came to appreciate the critical role which the developing Glencree Centre for Reconciliation could, did and does play. I spoke at various Glencree seminars and served as advisor on different initiatives. However, due to my many other engagements at home and abroad, I was never able to give it the time and attention I knew it deserved. I regret this but I also know that in the spirit of Glencree I am forgiven before I even confess.

In the midst of my other involvements, two aspects of the Glencree Centre and its activities stand out for me. The first of these is that it is a real centre with proper facilities including overnight accommodation for serious encounters even between the apparently irreconcilable. The second is the professionalism of its staff in mediating between the different and the difficult. These are the continuing achievements. The earlier vision faced with an isolated and dilapidated military barracks and a rather apathetic Irish society demanded courage and creativity, industry and persistence from the few if it was to be realised. Happily, that few proved equal to the task and attracted more and more support from public and government so that the Centre now plays an indispensable role in reconciling an Ireland so bitterly divided along political and religious lines for so long.

My hopes for Glencree are many. The reconciling task within Ireland between its traditional inhabitants as enemies is still far from complete. The recent regular work of Glencree's Irish encounters must continue to develop. The shifting political allegiances in Northern Ireland will need sensitive attention, analysis and mediation. The persisting paramilitary activity with its bases and perhaps targets in the Republic needs the kind of educational response for participants and supporters which Glencree may provide. Glencree can and perhaps already does help the new Irish immigration conflicts. It is becoming one our great challenges and may yet become our great shame. Our settler-Traveller conflicts continue but, unless I am mistaken, have not yet been seen as within Glencree's remit.

The religious divisions between Irish Catholics and Protestants were rightly seen and helpfully treated by Glencree as seriously contributing to the destructive political divisions. The religious and associated cultural plurality in Ireland is now rapidly increasing and demands new and greater efforts towards mutual understanding. Glencree has the spirit, the tradition and the resources to help tackle this and let the new plurality become a source of mutual enrichment rather than a source of mutual degradation. People of all religious allegiances and none in contemporary Ireland should have a forum where differences are discussed not with a view to eliminating them but with the goals of mutual understanding, mutual tolerance and mutual enrichment. Where probably all religious groupings, even the

Roman Catholic one, feel like threatened minorities, and this may apply even more to non-religious people, the practices of truth and freedom, justice and reconciliation need public encouragement, skilled personnel and a centre like Glencree to ensure the essential dialogue.

There is a much greater task than any mentioned already, important as these are, awaiting the reconcilers of Glencree and of the wider world. In a new century already riven by war, it might seem utopian to speak of the twenty-first century as that which might witness the abolition of war as a political instrument, as the nineteenth century witnessed the abolition of slavery as a political instrument. Yet as a new and remarkable book by Jonathan Schell (*The Unconquerable World: Power, Nonviolence and the Will of the People*, 2003) points out, there are strong negative and positive reasons why this may be possible and necessary. In this work he is recounting and analysing many of the non-violent achievements and insights of the twentieth century, from Gandhi to the end of colonialism, the fall of the Soviet Union, the end of apartheid in South Africa and the spread, however incomplete, of human rights and democracy. He outlines some of the possible developments of what he calls "co-operative power" which could gradually lead to its replacing "coercive power" as key to national and world politics. This brief and crude summary does scant justice to a complex and invigorating book, offering real hope in dark days.

Of course, this is not the only or first harbinger of the hope that the twenty-first century might see the last of the great barbarisms, war. Both intellectual and popular movements are busy with such ideas and ideals. I, along with a leading American theologian of Methodist background, Professor Stanley Hauerwas of Duke University, issued an appeal to Christian leaders and theologians in 2001 to work for the abolition of war in this century. Despite poor circulation of the appeal, it met with a good positive response. And there are many other examples of similar proposals from religious and secular sources. It does, however, seem that Glencree with its distinctive vision, experience and skills could play an important role in what is becoming a global movement, if still small. As think-tank, forum for debate (on a new Irish/EU foreign policy including security through reconciliation?) and training centre (for future peace-keepers?), Glencree could be a beacon not just for reconciliation and the elimination of violence in Ireland but in the wider world.

Colin Murphy

*Colin Murphy was born in Belfast in 1936. His family roots
are in Fermanagh, Antrim and the Isle of Man. After school
he first worked in accountancy and then in sales and market-
ing. He moved to Dublin in 1975 with his wife Margaret and
daughters Sheelagh and Lynne. Away from family and work,
Colin has had a lifelong interest in community development
and in finding ways out of conflict. This journey has led him
to involvement with a wide range of organisations and causes
which address these issues throughout Ireland and elsewhere.*

WHEN OUR END OF THE MURPHY family came to live
in Dublin in 1975, we had already had some involvement in so-called peace work. After the horrors of
post-1969 violence, Margaret and I made a conscious
decision to look out from our almost entirely Protestant
view of the world and engage with the "other", i.e. the
Roman Catholic/nationalist minority in Northern Ireland. That decision introduced us to many interesting
encounters: Women Together, PACE (Protestant and
Catholic Encounter), New Ulster Movement, Corrymela
Community, Inter-Church Emergency Fund for Ireland,
Ballynafeigh Clerical Fellowship, East Belfast Community Council, amongst others.

During this period, as the result of being in the office
of the Irish Council of Churches at the right time, I was
invited to participate in a study tour to the Netherlands

of so-called significant people involved in community activity at the time. (André Lascaris deals with this event and the subsequent establishment of the Dutch/Northern Irish Advisory Committee elsewhere in this book.) Suffice it to say that my experience with the "Dutch Committee" exposed me to political, cultural and "gospel" ways of looking at conflict that resonated with my own feelings and gave me a rationale that I could work with. I learned about scapegoating, the complexity of any given conflict and the negative effects that flow from the tendency of human beings to copy and rival each other. I learned to read the Bible, and especially the gospels, with new eyes. I learned to concentrate my mind and actions more on freedom and less on guilt; more on possibilities and less on problems; more on transforming conflict and less about escalating it; more about love and less about power games. I began to see Jesus as truly human and to learn about dealing with conflict by following his example: do the unexpected, go the extra mile, take a risk now and again, refuse to play the scapegoat game, love unconditionally, etc.

Then I came to Glencree.

I don't think anyone who knew the place would disagree that Glencree was running out of steam in the mid-1980s. The original Christian ecumenical vision was under pressure in a Centre where some staff and volunteers were promoting conflicting ideologies. The experiment of establishing a base in Belfast had gone wrong. The original concept of offering sanctuary and refuge to people from Northern Ireland was less relevant. There was great need to upgrade the facilities and, as ever, there was no money, rather a crippling debt.

That was the bad news. The good news was that the membership was largely still intact, the "brand" was still recognised and valued by civil society in the Republic and the peace education programme developed by James and Sarah McLoughlin on the Glencree farm continued to thrive.

The questions for council, members, staff and volunteers were clear: How do we save the place and the ideal? Can we struggle on? What about the debt? What is our task as a "peace" organisation? What are we going to do about all the conflicts within?

In the midst of this process, I found myself elected to the Chair. I recall very difficult meetings at the Centre and elsewhere, worried staff and volunteers, various fruitless attempts to deal with the cash crisis, increasingly impatient creditors and, above all, a sense that the organisation had lost its way. To cut a long story short, I decided to take a risk, close the place down, and thereby give ourselves as much time as we needed to work out if we should start again. The council of the day accepted the proposal and we duly paid off the staff, sent the volunteers home and closed the doors in the autumn of 1988.

My own position was something like this: We can't go on like this; we need to face up to the debt. We need to work out what exactly a peace centre in County Wicklow is supposed to do — apart, that is, from offering refuge to Northern Ireland people. We need advice on whether to stay on the site. We need time and resources of people and money to deal with all these issues. All the time I was convinced that the Republic of Ireland would need an autonomous organisation dedicated to peace-making and that the value of such a centre would someday be acknowledged.

I remember working out in my head that my job was to facilitate the questioning process. I believed that answers to all the questions would inform major future decisions and that these answers, however long it took to reach them, would be positive. My vision stopped there, for I had no idea what Glencree would actually do when it got going again. I was confident, however, that if, when and where Glencree ever got restarted, competent people would get involved and the peace-building potential of society in the Republic of Ireland would be realised.

So, we suspended council meetings and all activity to allow a small group of people to work on the future of the organisation. I was happy to go along with this group and to include old and new hands as and when they appeared. During this period, I confess that I was hesitant to accept the views of people who didn't make sense to me and I listened to people who did. I remember using the analogy of a rose bush that had not been pruned for years. It was growing all over the place and was not bearing any flowers. I saw that it was my job to wield a set of very sharp pruning shears so that the plant could be cut back to its roots before being fit to grow again. I kept in touch with council members, updated them from time to time and asked for their continued moral support.

We set about dealing with the debt. This process involved disposing of assets (a house in Belgrave Square in Dublin) and talking to the two banks that were covering most of the remaining debt. AIB Bank, who were our

major creditor, were most understanding. First of all,
they agreed to freeze interest on the considerable over-
draft and then, when we began to show them our plans
for a re-start, agreed to forgive a substantial element of
the debt, in return for repayment of the balance on a
phased basis. (In time, we honoured this arrangement
and remain happy customers of AIB.)

The other bank, which had entered into an arrangement with Glencree in 1974, was a more difficult case.
They were very upset that a peace organisation would
not honour its obligations and complained, reasonably,
that they had not been kept informed over many years.
We had a final acrimonious meeting which resulted in
them writing off the debt and telling us never to darken
their doors again. We made arrangements with the other
creditors, including the understanding Church of Ireland minister whose house in Belfast was used as a base
by Glencree, and we eventually opened the doors again
in 1994, free of debt.

Meantime, we decided to commission two arms-
length pieces of research that would give professional/
academic views on what the mission of a new Glencree
might be and whether or not we should remain on the
site in the valley above Enniskerry in the Wicklow
Mountains. These reports were funded directly by a
grant from The Ireland Funds and indirectly by the organisations that undertook to do the work at substantially reduced fees.

On the issues of mission and purpose, Professor Patrick Buckland of the Institute of Irish Studies at the University of Liverpool undertook to prepare a research paper for the organisation. Professor Buckland in turn

commissioned Stephen Rourke (later council member and Chair at Glencree) to do the fieldwork and prepare the raw data for the report.

In a nutshell, the report recommended that the Republic of Ireland would be wise to maintain Glencree as a "peace centre" whose mission would be "To build the peace in the Republic of Ireland and with its neighbours and to work for the building of a truly pluralist (inclusive) Ireland". The report was very clear on the absolute importance of the Republic facing up to its own responsibilities for the causes and, hopefully, for the eventual transformation, of the conflicts in Ireland. If the south could take this task seriously, the report argued, it might give up its self-appointed task of acting as consultants on issues of violence and peace to the people of Northern Ireland.

Meanwhile, Deloitte and Touche Management Consultants undertook to make recommendations on the future use by Glencree of the buildings it had occupied since 1974 and to prepare a business plan that would chart a course for the next five years. Again, this report was favourable and recommended that the historical, cultural and scenic resources at Glencree were worth preserving and developing. Deloitte and Touche further recommended a "three-legged" approach to this provision: conference/residential accommodation, coffee shop and craft village. (It is interesting 12 years later to note that substantial progress has been made on the first two of these objectives.)

The work involved in managing the process described above fell to a very small group of people in addition to those referred to above. Included in this list are

Máirín Colleary (later council member and CEO), Pauline Geoghegan, Anne O'Meara and Peggy Murphy. Co-operation Ireland, via their CEO Tony Kennedy, was very supportive and allowed us to "squat" in their Dublin office where Susan FitzGerald looked after administrative matters towards the end of the process. Una O'Higgins O'Malley and André Lascaris were constantly available to give advice, as were other current and former council members. John Kelly's help on matters legal and regulatory was especially helpful. Throughout this period I kept in close contact with Eleanor, Lady Wicklow. I was very keen to build a bridge between the "first" Glencree and whatever would succeed it and Eleanor was very supportive of this process. Rev John Morrow, a founder of both Corrymeela and Glencree, also gave advice at this time. I hope the many other people who helped during this period but whose names are omitted will forgive me.

A real surprise slowly dawned on me that the new Glencree that was being envisaged would have a pluralist identity and that its specific ecumenical Christian ethos would be lost. For someone whose inspiration for peace-building begins with the Christian gospel, this was an unexpected challenge. However, I thought and talked about the issue and came to the understanding that a truly autonomous organisation with no specific religious identity might be freer to tackle issues around religion that bedevil the conflicts in Ireland.

The process outlined above took the greater part of five years. At times I felt like giving up but there was always a voice at one meeting or another that argued that we take just one more step. I realised that many people (not, thankfully, Margaret, Sheelagh or Lynne), including trusted friends and colleagues, thought I was mad to even bother. I was told that "people" were talking behind my back about the unsustainability of the Glencree renewal project and even the need for a peace centre in the Republic. Nevertheless, we stuck it out and eventually called a council meeting at which we presented our recommendations for the new Glencree and sought and received retrospective approval for all decisions taken over the five-year gap in meetings! Council bought the deal and we set about opening the doors and searching for a new chief executive. This post was to be filled by Ian White who was then working with Co-operation Ireland.

We decided that one of the elements of the re-launch of Glencree would be to invite Chris McGimpsey, a Unionist politician from West Belfast, to avail of a visit to Dáil Éireann that was facilitated by Senator Fergal Quinn. By chance (!), Ian arranged that Chris was in the Dáil chamber on the very day that Taoiseach Albert Reynolds announced the signing of the Downing Street Declaration earlier that afternoon.

Thus, it could be said, the Irish peace process and the new Glencree were born on the same day.

Paul Murphy MP

The Rt Honourable Paul Murphy was appointed as Secretary of State for Northern Ireland on 24 October 2002. He was previously Secretary of State for Wales. A former lecturer in Government and History at Ebbw Vale College of Further Education, he was a member of Torfaen Borough Council from 1973–87 and became MP for Torfaen in 1987. In Opposition he was Shadow Spokesman on Welsh Affairs (1988–94), Northern Ireland (1994–95), Foreign Affairs (1995) and Defence (1995–97). After the 1997 Election he was appointed Minister of State at the Northern Ireland Office with specific responsibility for Political Development. Following the negotiation of the Good Friday Agreement he was appointed a Privy Counciilor in the 1999 New Year Honours. Mr Murphy is a member of the Royal Institute of International Affairs, former secretary of the Franco/British Parliamentary Committee and former treasurer of the Anglo/Austrian Society.

In Northern Ireland the issue of dealing with the past is quite properly coming to the top of the political agenda.

I'm delighted to have been asked by the Prime Minister to look at how we can move forward on this issue so that all can have a better future. I've already held a series of meetings with people with experience and expertise in this field and consultation will continue in the autumn. Already, I'm convinced that there is a will and a determination to make progress in Northern Ireland, and I'm sure that we will be making some positive announcements in the months ahead.

While we are very much at the start of this process in Northern Ireland, I am conscious that, for the last 30 years, Glencree has been working quietly and tirelessly behind the scenes, helping to break down the barriers which many thought insurmountable. This is hugely important and significant work.

I was very impressed when I visited Glencree in December 2002 and was honoured to participate in the opening of the Peace Resource Centre. I was immediately struck by the beauty and magnificence of the landscape in which the Centre's facilities are set, tucked away in the Wicklow hills. What was once an army barracks and a reform school now houses people dedicated to building peace and reconciling differences. Reconciliation among people is an absolutely essential element in resolving conflicts such as we witnessed in Northern Ireland. Much of this work has to go on quietly and with great patience and understanding. This is why the British and Irish Governments have supported Glencree's work for many years. From humble beginnings in difficult times, Glencree has built for itself an international reputation.

The British and Irish Governments are committed to the implementation of the Good Friday Agreement and to securing a lasting peace. We have made significant progress, but Governments and politicians cannot achieve these goals alone. They can only be achieved and maintained in an environment and context of mutual trust, where people can, and want to, reconcile their cultural, religious and political differences through dialogue, not through violence.

Northern Ireland has to find ways of dealing with the past which recognises the pain, grief and anger that people feel individually — but which also allows them to move forward collectively, better prepared to build for the future. Clearly, just as there is no such thing as an archetypal victim of the Troubles, there cannot be a "one-size-fits-all" approach to dealing with their legacy.

The programmes run at Glencree provide a unique opportunity for peace-building and reconciliation between communities throughout Ireland, north and south and from Great Britain. These programmes help all those who come here, those who look for help in coming to terms with a painful past, those who want to understand and change the prejudices that continue to blight our society, and those who seek to build a better future.

We are all shaped by history. For some, that history has brought pain, suffering and loss; for others it has sent them on the path of inflicting that pain, suffering and loss. For the many who come to Glencree it has brought them to a point where they want to write a different history. A history of peace and mutual understanding.

Sean Nolan

Fr Sean Nolan was born in Rockcorry, County Monaghan where his family had a long tradition in farming and community service. When he came back to Monaghan as a priest, he got a deep understanding of the local culture in that remote part of the Republic. Fr Nolan served as a teacher in St McCartan's College and later as a priest in Monaghan town and he is currently serving the parishes of Errigal Truagh.

IN THE PAST 20 YEARS, my priesthood has been served in the context of the troubles in Ireland and in the particular context of north Monaghan. It has been an effort to get people who had their backs turned against each other to turn around and face their neighbours. For me, the issues have always been to turn away from intolerance and violence and look for ways to implement the gospel of reconciliation.

My first introduction to cross-border peace work was with the Intereg programme which brought me into close contact with men of vision like Harford Robb and Colin Stutt. I began to develop a new approach to parish life based on the concept of lifelong learning. I had been aware of Glencree and was pleased to be asked to participate in the Churches' Programme there. Glencree's initiative in working in the border corridor (Derry, Down, Antrim, Armagh, Tyrone, Fermanagh, Donegal,

Sligo, Leitrim, Cavan, Monaghan and Louth. It was for me a really helpful intervention.

Visits to Glencree with my own parishioners and people from County Tyrone and West Belfast provided transforming experiences for all of us. The Gap of the North (north Monaghan and parts of Tyrone) has a very long history and I am convinced that there is much value in working through shared experiences of the communities in that part of Ireland.

Of course there is always the danger in the work that organisations like Glencree engage in, namely that they stay on the surface — the superficial level — and avoid going deep enough to reach the real, hard issues. However, I believe Glencree's contribution has been and can be significant. The culture of openness, searching, inclusivity and probing is very valuable to the healing process that we all must engage in over the coming generations.

A personal transforming experience for me was to hear at Glencree how Nelson Mandela had a true meeting with the grandson of Hendrik Verwoerd, the president of South Africa, who was the architect of apartheid and who had ultimate responsibility for Mandela's 28-year imprisonment. I quote it here with permission from Wilhelm Verwoerd's own account of that meeting:

> . . . on 28 September 1991, a wish of mine came true and I got the opportunity to meet Mr Mandela in person. A short conversation with Madiba (the familiar name for Mr Mandela) began when I received a short, but friendly handshake. With all the noise he didn't hear when I introduced myself. I left it like that. Jannie Momberg, the host, fortunately came to my

rescue, as he didn't want to let such an "historic opportunity" go by.

I can't remember how I expected Madiba to react. In any case, his first words caught me off guard: "How is your grandmother? When you see her again, if she won't mind, would you please convey my best wishes to her . . ." "Don't worry about the past, let us work together for a better future. . ." Coming from him, these words left a very deep impression. "As a Verwoerd you have a great advantage; when you speak, people will listen".[3]

This encounter illustrates my point of redemption and reconciliation and meeting the other. I look forward to working again with Glencree in my lifelong journey to integrate the beauty of the Gap of the North in a way that develops the beauty of its wonderful people.

---

[3] *My Winds of Change*, Wilhelm Verwoerd, Raven Press, 1997.

Sean O'Boyle

Sean O'Boyle was born in Ballymena, Northern Ireland, in 1968. He has worked as a teacher in Northern Ireland, Austria, Nepal and the Republic of Ireland and as a youth worker in both parts of this island. He joined the Glencree Centre for Reconciliation as part of the Youth, Schools and Community Programme Team in 2001 and has been a co-ordinator of International Programmes at the Centre since 2003.

GLENCREE CENTRE FOR RECONCILIATION? Where's that? What do they do there?" Such was my reaction when a friend showed me an advertisement for a job on the Programme Team at Glencree in the winter of 2000. To my embarrassment, I had never heard of the place before (and here's me thinking "Ah, see me heh, I know a lot about all this reconciliation malarkey!"). Having had an interest in, and, experience of, cross-community work in the North, through my work as a youth leader and teacher, as well as through my Church, and following a little sortie to the centre to check it out, it struck me that the Glencree set-up sounded both interesting and challenging.

I applied, attended the interview, didn't get the job. Then again, nobody else did, as Glencree had re-assessed the need for the post. Two months later, I received a phone call inviting me to work at Glencree as a Programme Co-ordinator. I took it and began in March 2001.

So this is where the Northern Mafia in "the south" hang out, I thought to myself as I started. Centre Direc- tor: northerner; housekeeping manager: northerner; both youth, schools and community programme co- ordinators: northerners; Churches' programme co- ordinator: northerner; bookkeeper: northerner; new youth, schools and community programme co-ordinator (yours truly): northerner. It seemed as if those from "north of the border, down Cookstown way" were tak- ing over the place and instantly reminded me of the pro- phetic words of local boy did good, Leonardo O'Cohen: "First we take the Aras, then we take Glencree . . ."

Looking through the lists of youth and school groups that have passed through this little sanctuary in the Wicklow Hills, whether they be young people from Bal- lycastle or Ballina, Glenbryn or Galway, one is always questioning oneself as to how the experience of engaging with "the other" may have affected them. My hope would be that they will have returned to their home communities with more open attitudes to "the other", whether that "other" be a Protestant, a Catholic, a Travel- ler, an asylum-seeker, a woman, a man, a person of col- our, an English person, an Irish person, a gay person . . .

Glencree has provided me with amazingly enriching experiences, both personally and professionally. My youth work with the organisation allows me the oppor- tunity to work with the leaders of tomorrow. Since the summer of 2003 I have taken on the task of co- ordinating international programme activity which do not necessarily fit into any of the current Glencree op- erational areas. This opportunity has again provided me with experiences that are inspiring and challenging and enables me to indulge my love of world politics and to link with my academic background in international development.

Sometimes, when Glencree people explain their work to friends or other interested parties, they get lauded with phrases such as, "Oh, what you do is amazing!" Very kind words. But I often feel that I am simply lucky to be at Glencree, to experience what takes place here, with an incredible team of colleagues and friends. We don't always get it right and, as one of my colleagues wisely reminds us time and time again, we don't have a monopoly on wisdom. However, hopefully we learn from our mistakes, learn from each other, and move off again in the right direction.

I have met many incredible individuals and organisations in the past three and a half years. Many of those have been inspirational to me and helped me realise how fortunate I have been to share in this "Glencree experience". Personally and professionally, it has been well worth the long trek, a trek on which I have been carried, and continue to be carried, by many special people.

Una O'Higgins O'Malley

Una O'Higgins O'Malley has dedicated her public life to the search for peace on the island of Ireland. She was one of the founding members of Glencree and has been involved for many years as council member, president and supporter. Una was instrumental in the development of the Glenstal Ecumenical Conference and is a former President of the Irish Association. Her memoirs, From Pardon and Protest *and an anthology of her poems,* Twentieth Century Revisited *were published by Arlen House in 2001 and 2003 respectively.*

Women at Glencree

WE WERE INDEED A MIXED BUNCH — we women who, together with a number of men, got together to make a reality of the dream of a Centre for Reconciliation at Glencree. But then that was what the new Centre was to be all about — unity in diversity.

To begin with, our ages were very different, ranging from quite elderly (but dynamic) ladies in their seventies to young girls from the Ballyfermot Peace Corps barely in their teens. Our social backgrounds also differed as indeed did our nationalities — some of the most memorable women in those early years were volunteers from abroad.

And then some were strongly motivated to try to spread peace because of their commitment to their religion while others wanted to hear nothing of Churches or

church-going. Feminism was developing apace in Ireland at the time; the Women's Political Association was
beginning to make an impact, Women's Aid was running hostels, one of which was next door to the Glencree
Office in Harcourt Street, with which we had
neighbourly relations. In particular (where Glencree was
concerned), 20 women's organisations had got together
to establish an umbrella group called the Women's Voluntary Association; such large groupings as the Irish
Countrywomen's Association, the Irish Housewives Association and the Association of Women's Clubs were
active in this Voluntary Association and consequently,
through their chairperson Lady Wicklow (formerly the
Labour Senator Eleanor Butler) who became a member
of the steering committee of Glencree, many of those
women also formed a commitment to Glencree. Concern
for people in the North suffering because of the troubles
there had brought these groups together and so they
were glad to see Glencree taking shape and hosting
Northern visitors (many of them women and children).

Some relics of their work for Glencree still remain —
the coloured blankets were knitted for the Centre by
Irish Countrywomen members. Other knitting and
weaving was done by visitors from abroad; I think of
Ellen, an American volunteer who gathered tufts of
sheep's wool from the fields round about and spun and
knitted them into items to be sold in the shop. But in
case you might think the first Glencree women were
confined to sewing and baking, I hasten to say I also remember Ellen working hard on the roof of the forge.

Memorable among the Northern women who supported Glencree at that time were Saidie Patterson, a dis-

tinguished trade unionist and a woman of great faith and courage. Herself a Protestant in her work for Women Together, she had made many friends among the Catholic members and she led a number of mixed groups southward — both to Glencree and before that to the hostel in Newbridge (lent to us by Irish Ropes) where we first welcomed visitors from the North. Saidie was someone to remember; her courage, determination and humour inspired us and helped us greatly. Through their shared commitment to the Labour movement, she and Eleanor Wicklow had formed a bond earlier in their lives which they were delighted to revive at this time.

Another remarkable Northern lady was Sister Anna, an Anglican nun known to many in Belfast for her bravery and energy. It was said she would fly through riots on her bicycle, her habit blowing in the wind, exhorting peace and non-violence! On a famous occasion in Dublin she must have mistakenly duplicated her list of visitors since two lots of weary Belfast people came to us though only one lot was booked in. The day was saved, however, by a white knight — or rather earl — since Eleanor's husband, Lord Wicklow, gallantly put up the extra guests in the penthouse of Jury's Hotel at his own expense.

At the younger end of the scale, there were workcampers — particularly the girls of the Ballyfermot Peace Corps and similar groups based in many Dublin parishes. Their generosity and hard work was amazing and they developed a love for Glencree which was very touching. Some called it their university — I think for me it was also that! Sarah McLoughlin, a neighbour, was another woman who did Trojan work for Glencree though her children were at that time very young. Her lovely character and disposition did much to establish peace and serenity at the Centre.

The Glencree of today is founded on much goodwill and on very many contributions from women — some of them heroic. For people like me who saw it in its early grimness it is the greatest pleasure to know that their generosity and belief in the cause have borne much fruit.

I offer these words as a 30th birthday present to Glencree:

The Old Barracks at Glencree

The old lady clutches her shawl of clouds around her
    bony shoulders
and gazes down the valley
hugging a dream that no one else can measure ;
one day she will be filled again, she knows,
though clamorous rooks make nurseries in her hair
and the prying sky gapes in through rotting rafters.

"I will house peace," she says, "a prince will come
from Wales to do me honour and I shall blend
the echoes of Welsh soldiers with sounds of children's
    laughter
and the distinctive accents of the North.

"Some will come here to pray," she says, "and some to
    build
and I shall reach them all because my bridge
will then be sturdy and I shall hold them in my house
in harmony."

And so she dreams in solitude and silence,
confident of her appointed destiny.

Twentieth Century Revisited, Una O'Higgins O'Malley, Arlen Press, 2002

Ivo O'Sullivan

Ivo O'Sullivan was born in Cork in 1927 in Cork of Kerry parents. In 1955 he was appointed Assistant Lecturer and subsequently Senior Lecturer in the Science Faculty of University College Dublin. In 1958–60 he worked as a Research Associate and Assistant Professor at Duke University, North Carolina and in 1975 was Visiting Lecturer (final term) at Njala College, University of Sierra Leone. In his spare time Ivo has been engaged in voluntary work, mainly, Legion of Mary and later Viatores Christi. In the 1970s Ivo was a member of the Irish Commission of Justice and Peace. In 1974, he was appointed a Member of the Royal Irish Academy. After retirement, he became an Associate of the Glenstal monastic community, active with the Family and Media Association, and associated with The Focolare movement.

Events leading to the Formation of the Glencree Centre for Reconciliation

WITHOUT MUCH RESEARCH, it would be difficult for a non-historian to record the momentous events of the period from the late 1960s and early 1970s which led to the formation of the Glencree Centre for Reconciliation.

However, major events which spring to mind (with the aid of documents and minutes of meetings, taken down from the attic, which I will leave with the Centre), include the civil rights movement in the North, followed by rights marches in Derry and a virtual pogrom in

Catholic areas of Belfast (August 1969). This was followed by the arrival of the British army with the intention of restoring order. The army was initially welcomed
by Catholics in these parts of Belfast. The continued violence and atrocities were of immense concern to all. The
Irish and British governments were faced with enor-
mous problems. But what could the ordinary citizen do?

The Bloody Sunday atrocity by the British army in
Derry on 30 January 1972 brought the whole country out
in protest. This was followed by the Bloody Friday
atrocity by the Provisional IRA in Belfast later that year,
on 21 July. In contrast — silence!

A number of members of Viatores Christi[4] were out
hiking in the Wicklow hills on the Sunday following the
latter event and it was discussed by a few of them along
the way. They felt that the silence had to be broken and
that they should do something about it. On the following few days contacts were made with a number of others and an informal group was formed.

The group decided to hold a demonstration outside
the Sinn Féin headquarters (at that time in Kevin Street,
Dublin). It took the form of a silent protest vigil from
5.00 pm, Friday 28 July to 1.00 pm on Saturday. This was
followed on the Monday with a peace walk, which
many people joined, from the Garden of Remembrance
to Christ Church Cathedral. There it linked with an interdenominational prayer meeting for peace organised

---

[4] Viatores Christi is an Irish Catholic lay missionary association
which prepares and finds assignments for volunteers to work, for an
average period of two years, in overseas areas of need.

by the Women's Voluntary Emergency Service (WVES)
led by the late (Lady) Eleanor Wicklow.

The group were obviously concerned by the loss of
life and the suffering of the bereaved and their families.
They were also concerned about the world-wide report-
age of the events and the scandal caused by Christians
tearing each other apart. The political situation in
Northern Ireland would not have been known or understood by many.

The informal group, all of whom were Catholics,
continued with other peace activities during the autumn
of 1972. They then decided to form a peace group which
would be Christian and interdenominational in character, and which was later named, "Working for Peace".

People who had participated in the protest vigil and
peace walk and others interested in pursuing further
peace work were invited, by means of a press release, to
a meeting on 14 October to discuss possible activities. As
a result, people of high calibre, both Catholic and of
various Protestant denominations, joined the organisation; others joined later. It was from this membership of
some 40 to 50 persons that the Glencree Centre for Reconciliation emerged.

The new Working for Peace (WfP) group set about
organising various activities. First, they had to educate
themselves and others in the theory and effective practice of peace and non-violent work. In this, they had in-
valuable assistance from Jerome Connolly, then Executive Secretary of the Irish Commission for Justice and
Peace and a member of WfP. He was the main organiser
of a seminar/teach-in weekend in December 1972 on
"Peace and Non-Violence". He later produced a list of

activities entitled "Peace is an Enterprise of Justice" for those wishing to engage in peace work, and on February 1973 he gave an extensive talk on "Peace Work in Ireland: Linking Theory and Practice".

The activities of WfP were later divided among a number of working groups; Dublin northside and southside active groups, a peace centre committee, a bridge-building group and a Peace Week committee. There were also joint activities such as public meetings and peace walks. An Executive Committee was elected with a rotating chairperson.

Some Notable Events

The first press conference was held in the Ormond Hotel in Dublin on 1 February 1973 to make WfP known to the public and to announce the holding of its first public conference on 14 February at the College of Technology, Kevin Street on the theme "Peace and the People". This was one of three public conferences held during that year. The first Peace Week was held from 10 to 17 March.

A Reconciliation Walk was held, with the help of others, on 12 December 1974 to express sympathy and support to the bereaved in the recent bombings in Dublin and Monaghan, in Birmingham and earlier in the North. Attendance was estimated at 14,000 (others put it at 40,000).

A second peace walk was held on 15 January with the theme "Let the Ceasefire be Permanent — Let us work for Reconciliation and Justice". We were appalled when the ceasefire ended the following day. A third peace walk was held three days later. Rev Ray Davey was organising a demonstration against the resumption of hostilities on 19 January in Belfast and requested support from Dublin. So WfP organised a third peace walk on the same day in Dublin. (The ceasefire was headline news and the peace walk was mentioned in reports so further publicity was not required.) 15,000 people participated.

The Peace Centre

At the teach-in on December 1972, Una O'Higgins O'Malley suggested considering the possibility of starting a Corrymeela-type peace centre[5] and it was agreed to look into this. In the meantime, through her contacts, a visitors' hostel belonging to the Irish Ropes company in Newbridge was offered to WfP in April 1973, on a temporary basis, to be used to give respite to those living in areas of stress in the North.

A committee was set up under Una's chairmanship to run the Centre. The Centre was opened by Ray Davey on the Saturday of Easter Week in the presence of the then Minister for Foreign Affairs, Dr Garret FitzGerald and some 80 people including the Chairman and MD of Irish Ropes, members of the Newbridge Council, of the local community and other interested groups. The first guests from the North had arrived the previous day.

The Centre was used until mid-October. Ten groups of about ten people came for ten-day rest periods and they expressed their heartfelt gratitude. The Newbridge project was acknowledged to have been a great success

[5] The Corrymeela Community is a scattered interdenominational Christian community that maintains a centre in Ballycastle, County Antrim, founded in 1965 by Rev Ray Davey, a Presbyterian minister.

and it encouraged WfP to continue looking for a permanent peace centre.

The Executive Committee had formed a Reconcilia-
tion Centre Steering Committee in July 1973, to search
for a suitable premises. The Committee, chaired by Rev
Denis Cooke (Methodist), included Lady Wicklow of
WVES and Victor Bewley of the Society of Friends;
Frank Purcell acted as Secretary.

Several sites and premises were inspected and found
unsuitable and finally the old reformatory at Glencree,
County Wicklow was inspected by Andrew Devane, Architect, and was found to have possibilities. The reformatory was in the care of the Office of Public Works and
after negotiations, with the support of the Minister for
Finance, it was *pro tem* put in the charge of WfP in November 1973 to enable work to proceed at the reformatory. The Steering committee had much work to do concerning finance, insurance, renovation plans, personnel
to run the Centre, etc.

As work continued at Glencree, there was much discussion over the following months about the Articles of
Association of Glencree. One of the important issues discussed was whether the Glencree Centre should remain
principally under WfP management or that it should be
managed by a body independent of WfP. In April 1974, it
was decided that Glencree should be an autonomous
body. WfP nominated the first nine members of its
Council, which would then co-opt representatives of
other peace organisations. The one condition enjoined on
the elected members of WfP was to ensure that the Centre would remain Christian and interdenominational in
character. The reformatory was then leased to the Glen-

cree Centre for Reconciliation for 99 years in the spring of 1994. The Centre was officially opened in May 1975.

Una O'Higgins O'Malley was a member of the Steering Committee and it was largely due to her determination, selfless commitment, perseverance and contacts that the Centre became a reality. Of course, it was also due to all who gave generously of their time and talents to the enterprise, and who persevered in keeping the Centre going, through many difficult circumstances, so that it has become "a place for peace" and an inspiration and encouragement to many.

To conclude, let me quote from a few early documents of the movement.

The first time the public was invited to the Centre was for a tree-planting ceremony on 10 March during Peace Week 1974. It was performed by Ray Davey, who said, among other things:

> This country of ours, both north and south, cherishes many symbols. But, alas, too often they speak of the past and they tend to keep us looking back instead of forward. I think of a prayer by a great Scottish theologian, "Let not the past ever be so dear to us as to set a limit to the future . . ." The planting of a tree speaks — of the future, of growth, of growth, of new life, or new possibilities, of hope, and of what can be. It expresses the cry of the heart from the vast majority of the people of all of this land that there should and must be peace.

Taking a quotation from "Peace — the Desperate
Imperative" by Sodepax:[6]

> The word shalom, as it is used in the Bible, ex-
> presses the wholeness of full human life in a
> community of mutual sharing and affirmation. It
> . . . belongs to personal fulfilment. For a commu-
> nity it means the flowering of its common life in
> all respects. It is the fulfilment of the promises of
> God. . . . Justice means the establishment of the
> disadvantaged in the full rights and possibilities of
> their humanity. . . . We believe, however, that
> [these definitions] may be helpful to men of all
> faiths and of none, in discerning what makes for a
> full human community in our time.

---

[6] The Committee on Society, Development and Peace which was established by the World Council of Churches and the Pontifical
Commission for Justice and Peace.

Frank Purcell

Frank Purcell was born in Melbourne in 1931, of Irish descent. He became a priest of St Columban's Missionary Society in 1955, taught at the Columban seminary in Sydney for two years before going to Japan. In 1970, he was appointed to the General Council of the Columbans, based in Dublin. After three years, he resigned and became involved in reconciliation work at Glencree. He returned to Australia in 1976 and married Margaret in 1978. He became involved in the local Aboriginal Reconciliation Group which sought to challenge racist attitudes among mainstream Australians, and later worked on similar challenges arising from Muslim refugees in the area. Frank finished his working life lecturing in Australian Politics at La Trobe University Campus, Shepparton, Victoria. Now retired, he is working on a PhD thesis on the challenges facing Muslim migrants.

GLENCREE WAS OVERCAST, GRIM and silent on an autumn day in 1973. Una O'Malley, Judy Hayes, Marie O'Reilly and I were members of the Working for Peace group given the job of finding a place for a Reconciliation Centre. As we looked through its locked iron gates, we knew we had found the spot.

The Working for Peace group had begun as a protest against the IRA's Belfast bombings earlier that year. Brian Nelson and his wife Jackie held a 24-hour vigil outside Sinn Féin headquarters in Dublin. Others were moved to action by his protest and about 40 people

formed the Working for Peace group. Half were Protes-
tants, including the Methodist Minister at Leeson Park
Church, Dennis Cooke, Presbyterian Chaplain at Trinity
College, John Morrow and well-known Quaker leaders
Victor and Rachel Bewley. The other half were Catholic,
all laity, but among them well-known figures like Ivo
O'Sullivan and Jerome Connolly.

The Working for Peace people believed that an effective non-violent path had to be found to reconciliation in
Ireland. Members of the group had been inspired by the
efforts at Corrymeela in the North — an initiative of
Presbyterian Minister Ray Davey. Our group wanted to
develop a sister centre in the Republic.

How come an Australian was involved in such a project? At the time I was a member of the Columban international leadership team based in Dublin. Jerome Connolly, Executive Officer for the Catholic Commission for
Justice and Peace was one of those who had joined
Working for Peace. It was his initiative which resulted in
my becoming involved.

The group had decided to gather on Pentecost Sunday in the Irish Ropes Factory at Newbridge. It was an
acknowledgement of that company's support for reconciliation. They had lent us their hostel to accommodate
our Northern visitors seeking support and refuge.

Some of the Catholic organisers of that Pentecost
gathering were aware that if there were no Mass, many of
the Catholics would slip away for an hour or so to go to
Church. This would only highlight the divide between
Catholic and Protestant on a day we hoped to join together with the Spirit to seek non-violent alternatives. The
solution: I was invited to say Mass for the group.

John Morrow, a Presbyterian Minister, and a member of the Corrymeela Community, was among the participants. He and I planned the joint service. We shared a Liturgy of the Word, but John urged me to continue with a Eucharist so that the Catholics could fulfil their Sunday obligation.

When we came to the Communion, I noticed that the lay Protestant participants were lining up to receive. At the time, the Vatican had all kinds of prohibitions on giving Communion to non-Catholics, and still does. But on Pentecost Sunday, at a gathering of Irish Christians, it would have been quite un-Christ-like to refuse a share in the Lord's supper to people who publicly acknowledged Jesus as Lord and Saviour. So I gave communion to all who fronted up. Many of the Catholics told me later of their sense of relief at my decision.

That incident was a moment of truth for me. It was also one of the events in the early days of Working for Peace which won my support for the theme of "respect", respect for one another's religious and cultural traditions. That was the key principle on which we built our reconciliation strategies in those early days.

But, to go back to Glencree. All of us at the gates of Glencree knew that we had found the place for our centre. And so it came about.

As an Australian, I was surprised to learn some time later of a fascinating Australian connection with Glencree. Michael Dwyer was one of the last of the rebels of the 1798 Rising. He surrendered to the British army in the grounds of Glencree. The terms of his surrender were that he would be exiled to America. Instead he was transported to Australia.

But there was symbolism in Michael Dwyer's presence at Glencree. His was a rebellion in which both Catholics and Protestants had joined together to find a solution to Ireland's problems. At Glencree once again, Catholic and Protestant would join forces to find reconciliation and peace in Ireland.

My role for the next three years was to assist in getting Glencree turned into a Reconciliation Centre. I worked out of an office in Harcourt Street provided by Joe McMenamin, a property developer. Padraig Cannon gave us access to his photocopier in his office nearby.

I had two effective full-time partners in Una O'Malley and Judy Hayes. The hours they put in negotiating deals with the Office of Public Works, merchant banks and building firms as well as organising major street marches, Peace Week activities, lobbying governments in Dublin, London, Belfast and Washington and working with friends in the USA setting up the Ireland Fund was incredible. Somehow they managed to balance husbands, kids, dogs, horses and this reconciliation challenge. It was an eye-opener for me, coming as I did from the rather protected and privileged world of a Catholic priest.

But the unsung hero of the early development was a Jesuit priest, Shaun Curran. He volunteered to staff the centre while renovations and a refitting took place. That meant living in a lonely caravan just inside the gates for over three years. He was a volunteer funded and supported by the Irish Jesuits who saw the importance of what was being attempted in Glencree.

We were also supported by another early volunteer, a Grail member from the United States, Elizabeth Magee. She handled the office work and gave us the freedom to work on a range of reconciliation activities. Meetings with Sinn Féin, the British Embassy, various Loyalist and Republican groups in the North, going to the States to help set up the Ireland Fund — it was a whirl of activity, meetings and a liberating spiritual journey for us all.

And the committee was quite extraordinary. Rachel Bewley handled the programming and catering development needed as groups began to use the Centre. Eleanor and Billy Wicklow, Pat and Lil Collins, Lovell Parker and Bill McCullough, Dennis Cooke and John Morrow were all heavily involved in strategic planning and financial support roles.

But the most memorable event for me was a Reconciliation Church Service at Leeson Park Methodist Church. The Scripture readings were given by the sons and daughters of families who had fought on opposite sides during the Civil War. Members of the O'Higgins, Fitzgerald, Childers and Lemass families all participated in the readings and prayers. President Childers was a Protestant, the others Catholics. And, to the real surprise and delight of the gathering, as if in answer to the challenge of reconciliation, Eamon De Valera himself appeared just before the service began and took a seat with the participants. It was a stunning demonstration of what non-violent pathways could lead to, in spite of a bloody beginning.

It convinced me of what might be possible in the North if the process of reconciliation could be supported and sustained. That's the role Glencree was intended to play. Well done to all those who have made it continue to happen.

Stephen Rourke

*Stephen Rourke is an independent consultant in the voluntary
and community sector in Ireland. He was director of The Ireland Funds for a three-year period and is currently a non-
executive director of Philanthropy Ireland and Dublin AIDS
Alliance. He has been a member of the council of Glencree since
1992 and was Chairperson from 1997 to 2002. He was born in
Limerick in 1957. Stephen has lived, studied and worked in
both parts of Ireland — living in Ballymena from 1966 to 1976,
studying in Trinity College Dublin from 1977 to 1980, involved in community work in Belfast from 1981 to 1985 and
based in Dublin for the past 20 years with an active involvement in cross-community and cross-border activities.*

M Y EXPERIENCE OF LIFE HAS inevitably made me very
conscious and aware of the problems and difficulties which have afflicted this small island of ours over
the period of "the Troubles" and the subsequent out-
working of the Good Friday Agreement.

In particular, my own life experience has served to
emphasise the need for any peace agreements or peace
settlements to involve the active engagement of local
communities and local residents within all parts of Ireland, north and south. Without this buy-in from the
broad population of Ireland, any proposed peace settlements are doomed to failure.

Within this context, the work being carried out by the Glencree Centre for Reconciliation and sister organisations (such as Co-operation Ireland and the Corrymeela Community) is of critical importance. These organisations provide the opportunity and space for people to discuss and to reflect upon issues relating to peace-building, reconciliation, consensus, inclusivity, etc. Given that 10,000 people have been involved in peace-building at Glencree over the ten years, it is reasonable to assume that they have influenced two or three of their relatives and friends and that consequently over 200,000 people have been affected by the work of Glencree.

In addition to there numerical outcomes, Glencree has been a symbol and a focus for peace-building work in the Republic of Ireland. Naturally, the main concentration for this work has been focused within Northern Ireland, which has borne the brunt of the very many violent and horrific incidents that have taken place since 1969. However, this emphasis on the situation within Northern Ireland should not be used an excuse or a rationale for people in the Republic of Ireland to duck their responsibility to find ways to contribute to the peace-building process. Glencree has provided opportunities for people from within the Republic to engage in peace-building programmes and to identify ways in which they might complement work that is being done in Northern Ireland (i.e. through the Glencree political dialogue initiative and the work with victims/survivors and ex-combatants) and within Britain (e.g. the linkages which have taken place with the Warrington project).

Glencree should continue to try to engage with as many people as possible around issues relating to reconciliation, human rights and social justice. With the new facilities that have been developed at the Centre over the past five years, it is reasonable to assume that the organisation could carry out work with up to 20,000 people each year. This work is likely to embrace a particular focus on multiculturalism and relationships between the indigenous Irish population and people form other countries who have migrated to Ireland over the past five years (with this pattern of inward migration likely to become a noticeable trend within Irish society for the foreseeable future).

In much the same way as Glencree has created space and opportunities over the last 30 years for people and groups to discuss issues concerning Northern Ireland and relationships between the islands of Ireland and Britain, it is hoped that Glencree will also focus in the future upon the challenge of creating a truly intercultural and inclusive civil society in Ireland. Through the development of programmes and projects aimed at promoting greater mutual understanding and respect between all groups and individuals who inhabit the island of Ireland, Glencree can continue to build upon its achievements of the past 30-year period.

John Shiels

John Shiels was born in Belfast but lives in Dublin. He and his wife Maeve met when both were students at Queen's University; both subsequently became substantially involved with Glencree. Maeve has been a Council Member and chair of Glencree Women's Project. John has been a public servant (for three- to five-year periods each) in both jurisdictions in Ireland. The bulk of his 40-year career, however, has been in overseas development, involving work in or travel to 74 countries, interspersed with periods at home working, one way or another, in the context of the conflict in Ireland. He founded Annesley Resource Partnership in 1997; the group provides advisory, funding, training, project management and evaluation services primarily in the reconciliation field in Ireland.

Glencree? It's a reconciliation centre, one of the original two in Ireland. One of its distinguishing features is that it conducts most of its programme activities at the residential centre that it has been developing in the Wicklow Hills, south of Dublin, since 1974.

I have evaluated a number of Glencree programmes and projects at different times, most recently the political programme. I have been impressed, and surprised, at the extent to which the remote setting of the Centre has proven to be very acceptable to (particularly Loyalist) paramilitaries, politicians and political representatives. The setting that Glencree offers for serious and very con-

fidential exchanges justifies totally the 1994 decision not
only to resurrect Glencree after some years of decline
but also to remain physically at the Centre in the Wicklow Mountains.

At the time, as a member involved in the discussions,
I was not convinced of the necessity or wisdom of retain-
ing the buildings. Numerous Irish reconciliation agencies
(Irish School of Ecumenics, INCORE, Co-operation Ireland, Mediation Network of Northern Ireland, Future
Ways Project at the University of Ulster) contribute excellent work without burdening themselves with large residential centres. There was a danger that the needs of the
physical buildings would soak resources, funds and creative energy away from the real task.

But I was wrong. Glencree's own contribution would
not be the same if it was not where it is and this view is
widely held among many of those who have been very
close indeed to the conflict.

Each of Glencree's major programme interventions
brings its own particular ethos and value scale to the
table. Our evaluations have shown that when these are
mixed with Glencree's own culture and way of doing
things, participants regard the total offering as very acceptable. We have further found that northern participants tend to see possibilities at Glencree that are not
replicated in their own part of the world. Again, because
of the existence and location of the Centre, Glencree has
been able to more energetically address the crucial west/
east axis than other similar agencies. To its credit, Glencree has right from the start sought to articulate a role
for the south in the ongoing peace process. This willingness to articulate the Republic's role and tasks, coupled

with its firm location in Wicklow, creates a powerful multiplier in terms of its effectiveness. If Glencree was located, for instance, in mid-Tyrone, its work would be 25 per cent as significant as it is. The simple fact that it speaks from south of the border, I believe, magnifies that voice north of it.

Shortly before Glencree's near-collapse in the late 1980s/early 1990s, I feared for a time that focus and direction had been lost. I remember a particularly sad weekend at the Centre when one excellent gentleman with a long beard attempted to convince me that the way to peace in Northern Ireland was through the production of organic vegetables at Glencree. This episode helped me to formulate Shiels' Sixth Law, which states that a move into organic carrots is the penultimate step in the life-cycle of any institution other than an organic farm.

In my view, no peace will endure on this island unless, in addition to a political settlement, the ocean of suffering which the private armies inflicted on us since 1968 is addressed, rather than being professionally air-brushed from our collective memory. The way that Glencree addresses this issue, not only with the victims, but also with many of those who inflicted this suffering, requires and demonstrates a great deal of moral courage.

Over the years, Glencree raised for me something of a conundrum about the extent of its involvement in conflicts overseas. Shades of David Trimble's comment that when faced with a choice of "solving Northern Ireland" or solving the world, many of us will select the softer option. At least three of the substantial Irish peace and reconciliation agencies that I have worked with found the going tough at home, so got busy overseas prematurely. Glencree has started very convincingly, but very recently, as a spin-off of the Good Friday Agreement, after regions like Sri Lanka or Palestine/Israel actually requested Irish help. Now the time is absolutely right for Glencree to help address these conflicts and I hope that this activity will develop significantly.

I recently re-read Theodore Roosevelt's dictum:

> It is not the critic who counts, not the man who points out how the strong man stumbles. . . .The credit belongs to the man who is actually in the arena, whose face is marked by dust and sweat and blood.

To mix my metaphors, the rest of us are the hurlers on the ditch, but it is Glencree and its people who are in the arena.

Sonja Tammen

Sonja Tammen, 38, is a journalist from Hamburg. Her mother was a teacher and her father a railway worker and she spent her childhood in the small mid-western German town of Hann, Meunden. Looking for adventure, Sonja left home 20 years ago, first working in a kindergarten before going to Hamburg to study political science, history and Swedish. Her activities in the anarchistic and feminist movements at college resulted in Sonja delaying the completion of her studies until she was 29. Since then, Sonja has worked for a variety of TV magazines and has produced a political radio show. In 2004, she took six months off to work as a volunteer at Glencree.

A FTER FIVE YEARS WORKING AS a TV magazine journalist, I was looking for new experiences. So I took six months off from my job and went to Glencree in Ireland. The Centre for Reconciliation seemed to be the ideal place for a political-minded person like me to learn more about the Troubles, to do some hands-on work, and to meet interesting people.

I came in May, when the Wicklow Mountains were brown and the countryside looked like an amazing moonscape, with breaks of small wooded areas and a lot of brave sheep who used the roads for a rest. Then the breathtaking arrival: the old barracks of Glencree, the wonderful view from the mountains down the valley, the beautiful Sugar Loaf and, in the distance, the sea.

At Glencree I've had a lot of experiences, both personally and politically. We volunteers have a very basic
life. Our role is to let the visitors feel good, clean the
rooms, prepare the meals and help wherever we can. We
live close together, share our bedrooms, and the volunteer kitchen is, most of the time, a disaster. We haven't
chosen each other, and sometimes it needs a lot of tolerance to accept the different ways of being and working,
the loud music, the bad moods . . . and in such an isolated place as Glencree, it is difficult to escape. On the
other hand, I learn a lot from the volunteers who are
from different countries and cultural backgrounds. I am
sure that I will miss this special family feeling when I
am back in my brain-isolating single flat in Hamburg.

Politically, I can't believe how much I have learnt
here. I have met great people from Israel/Palestine and
South Africa, from the Basque Country and Belgium,
victims and ex-prisoners from Northern Ireland, Great
Britain and the Republic of Ireland, community groups,
Travellers, the women's group, politicians from every
side, church representatives, school students, ecological
groups and a lot of interesting individuals.

To speak with survivors of the Troubles in the LIVE
programme was the most impressive experience for me.
I am full of respect for their way they manage their pain
as a part of their life. From them, I heard a lot of horrific
stories: for example, about a husband who was killed in
Belfast just two months before the ceasefire, or about a
brother who was killed in a bank robbery in Dublin.
Some of the participants were directly hurt by bomb at-
tacks. Every story is different; every person suffers in
their own way. Family and friends at home seemed to be

the wrong people to speak to about their traumatic events. But here at Glencree, the participants use the possibility to talk and reflect with people in similar situations. Because of these courageous people, I start to think that the best way to manage traumatic experiences is to make peace with your enemies, because if you are full of hate you only hurt yourself and can't challenge your hard life in a positive way.

Another group who changed my political point of view were the ex-prisoners. I met sensitive people, deeply engaged in the peace process in their communities. Maybe without these people and their paramilitary background, a peaceful development could not materialise. On the other hand, these ex-prisoners may be responsible for the suffering of a lot of people. A difficult duality. When I arrived at Glencree, it was unbelievable for me that (earlier) enemies like Republican and Loyalist paramilitaries, the police and British military can spend time fruitfully together. Now I know more about the backgrounds of these groups, and it is a new experience for me to allow myself to understand all sides of this conflict. That does not mean I tolerate the behaviour of the different people or groups, but my opinion is more complex than it was before, because now I see the dynamic of political violence and the deep injury of people who are involved in this conflict. Hopefully, I have learned to be more tolerant in political conflicts than I have been, for example, in Hamburg.

But there are more problems on this island than the Troubles. There is, for example, the discrimination against the Travelling community in the Republic of Ireland. And like in Germany there is the big issue of racism in Ireland. In June 2004, the Irish people voted in a referendum that children of immigrants, who are born in the Republic, will not automatically be Irish citizens. I would be happy if Glencree would work more on this issue. Nevertheless, racism is sometimes included as a theme in the programmes, but I feel it should play a more significant part.

Another lesson I learned more about in Glencree is the way to facilitate groups. Sometimes the only thing the programme people are doing here is to bring people together. And this simple method of facilitation can be so successful! The facilitator supports the different people in their way of thinking or makes this thinking understandable for the group, without bringing in his or her own position. And that means the facilitator must hear very clearly what the participants are saying. For me it is a learning process, to really hear what the person next to me is talking about.

Being a politically minded person, it is important for me to comment on the structures at Glencree. A lot of things work very well, but there is a very definite hierarchy and sometimes people don't get the respect they deserve. Glencree as an organisation needs to be more open-minded and to improve its internal communication. This will increase opportunities and solve most of the problems I have encountered.

Here in the Wicklow Mountains I've met a lot of amazing people. Three months after my arrival, the landscape has changed. The trees are full and dark, the ferns move like soft green waves in the wind and the heather already shows the first gentle purple flowers.

Melanie Verwoerd

*Melanie Verwoerd was born in Pretoria, South Africa in 1967.
In the early 1980s, she began her studies for a BA degree in
theology in Stellenbosch University and went on to receive an
MA degree in Feminist Theology in 1996. During her visit to
Oxford in 1986 she began making links with political organisations and on her return to South Africa in 1990, became a
member of the ANC. In 1994 she was elected as ANC Member
of Parliament, making her the youngest female member. During her seven years in parliament, as a member of fact-finding
teams, she visited Holland, Australia, Cuba, Sweden, Chile,
Brazil, the USA, Taiwan, Israel and Ireland. In March 2001
she was appointed South African Ambassador to Ireland.
Melanie is married to Wilhelm and they have two children.*

I HAD HEARD ABOUT GLENCREE via Dr Van Zyl Slabbert
in South Africa before I came to Dublin in 2001. I
made a note to get in touch when, coincidentally, I noticed a request from Ian White for a telephone contact
back home lying on a desk in the embassy. I used this
pretext to call Ian and make an appointment to visit the
Centre. I remember that it was a cold day and my husband and I resolved to make the visit brief. We ended up
spending most of a day there. That visit resulted in a
continuing connection, involving, amongst other things,
my husband Wilhelm joining the staff to take responsibility for Glencree's work with ex-combatants.

I was struck then by the beauty of the place and the
ease with which one could engage with the people there
and with their exciting and inspirational programme
activities. Glencree, through Ian, was also very helpful
in making arrangements for the embassy to use the Centre facilities for staff workshops. I was pleased to be
asked to deliver the keynote address at a Glencree Business Club function in Dublin Castle and to deliver the
annual women's lecture at the Summer School in 2002.

My experience in South Africa has convinced me of
the importance of having places like Glencree where
people on either side of a divide can meet, shake hands
and look each other in the eye. These encounters are essential to any conflict transformation endeavour and
have been central to my personal experience and to that
of my husband.

During my time as ambassador to Ireland, many important two-way links have been established with Glencree. I was pleased that the He'atid young leaders'
group was facilitated there and that the Buskaid young
people's orchestra from Soweto were so happy and comfortable during their visit to Ireland to celebrate the
tenth anniversary of freedom in South Africa. The embassy has also in a limited way helped to facilitate visits
of Glencree programme participants to wilderness experiential training in South African. I know that these visits have involved former combatants and survivors of
the conflicts in Ireland living together in the bush and
that the experiences that they shared have been thera-
peutic and creative for them.

I wish Glencree well with its programme work and
with the continual struggle to make the buildings com-

fortable — but not too comfortable! — for participants. The patient work that happens in places like this goes largely unnoticed and unsung in a world where peace-building is very much a "minority sport". In this respect there are many similarities with my own country. I can no more than trust that governments and civil society support the visionaries who struggle to make these places available for purposes of conflict transformation, wherever they exist.

I look forward to more peace-building partnership work with Glencree.

Wilhelm Verwoerd

Since May 2002 Wilhelm Verwoerd has co-ordinated the "(Ex)-combatants" Programme at Glencree. During this time he co-facilitated three visits of (potential) participants in various Glencree programmes to South Africa, with an emphasis on wilderness work. Before he came to Ireland in 2001, as the husband of the South African Ambassador to the Republic of Ireland, he was a philosophy lecturer at the University of Stellenbosch. He also served as a researcher on the South African Truth and Reconciliation Commission.

Troubled Scatterlings in a South African Wilderness

TWELVE BUFFALOES BRIEFLY GREETED us on that cloudy afternoon as we entered the Umfolozi wilderness area. Our guide, Bruce, later described this encounter as a "meaningful coincidence". In Zulu culture, he explained, the buffalo is a symbol of community. When a herd of browsing cattle becomes too scattered, the herd-boy burns buffalo dung, and somehow the smell draws the herd together again. I am inclined to agree with Bruce. Looking back on the five days that our motley crew of 12 recently spent in that unspoilt corner of South Africa — a former RUC man, two Loyalist and two Republican ex-prisoners, a former prison warder, a nationalist community worker, a camera man, two facilitators and two guides — it would seem that the smells and the sounds . . . and the silence of that wilderness indeed, gently, encircled these scatterlings of the Troubles. Don't get me wrong. I am not suggesting that this was a romantic, tension-free peace mumbo in an African jungle. There were no extended group hugs around the campfire. But something did happen during those days of walking, sitting, sleeping on the naked skin of the cradle of humankind. And I think whatever happened has something to do with the meaning that Bruce saw in that unexpected encounter with the buffaloes. As we were about to leave the wilderness area, with a small herd of impala and a family of zebra running away in the distance, he made us sit down under a few trees. Then, with a quiet voice, he shared his deep concern about the tragic ways in which we humans are divided by culture. And he conveyed the hope that the last few days in Umfolozi not only helped us to rediscover our connectedness as humans, but also to *experience* our shared membership of the fragile community of Life.

Reflecting on this Umfolozi experience I slowly began to see some of the ways in which our group was invited to become less scattered.

A Shared Vulnerability

No matter how tough you are, whether you are a man or a woman, black or white, Loyalist or Republican . . . when you enter a Big Five wilderness area on foot, you tend to feel rather vulnerable. The Big Five — elephant, lion, rhino, buffalo and leopard — are so-named because they are the most dangerous animals to hunt, and they are all there. During the day, one is easily lulled into a false sense of security coming across their tracks and drinking holes, walking past heaps of dung, or touching the worn bark where rhino or buffalo or elephant have scraped dried mud and ticks off their hides. Sometimes one sees these huge animals in the distance; rarely one feels the need to call for the protection of the seasoned guide with his gun. This sense of security quickly evaporates, however, when you have to cross a muddy river where crocodiles are known to lurk; or when you go to fetch water from the river, and suddenly there is a rhino walking up the same track.

It is in the small hours of the night, when one is alone on night watch, with nothing but a small fire and a torch, that the presence of the Big Five (and especially the predators among them) truly brings home one's primal vulnerability as a clawless, pampered human being. You also become deeply aware of your responsibility to remain vigilant for the sake of the even more vulnerable sleeping members of the group.

The sharing of night watch duties among the members of our group — with a prison warder and a policeman being protected by former politically motivated prisoners *and* vice versa — can be seen as a poignant symbol of a different, less divided kind of community. A community where, even in the absence of the Big Five, everyone remains humbled by a sense of human vulnerability; a community in which our shared responsibility to protect the vulnerable is not forgotten.

Intruders and Predators

It was a picture of peacefulness. I was sitting quietly, perched on top of a cliff above the White Umfolozi river, enjoying a time of safe solitude. Below me the African sun was baking down on a small herd of buffalo, some taking their siesta on a few sandbanks in the middle of the river, others snoozing away in the swallow water. Except for a few tails slowly chasing flies away and the bright ripples in the breeze, there was little movement. Suddenly, the one buffalo nearest to the far side bank looked up and reluctantly, lazily, got to his feet. Others followed, and then the whole herd started to run away, sploshing noisily through the water to a place of safety.

I eagerly looked around to see what scared these huge creatures away. I was expecting a pride of lions or some other serious predator. Then I saw a piece of blue moving in the distance. Pointing my binoculars in that direction, a few humans — members of another small group of scatterlings — came into focus.

So, just a whiff of human presence was enough to send those huge, dangerous creatures running for cover. The same thing happened the next day. This time a few rhino were sent scrambling for safety when they got our scent. Watching these rhino run away from us and witnessing the buffalo's peace being disturbed really made me feel like an intruder. Thinking back at the long distance we had to travel to come to this rare wild place — and even here we sometimes could hear an aeroplane or from a hilltop on a distant horizon see signs of ever-encroaching human settlements — reminded me that those animals had good reason to be scared.

Some members in our group carried open scars of the great scattering typically referred to as "the Troubles". The more hidden injuries of others, often made even less visible by the label of past imprisonment, have tempted many to distinguish between "victims" and "perpetrators". These distinctions tend to keep us humans scattered. However, the shattered peace of those buffalo invite us to look beyond what we have done to each other as human beings, to remember another deep, humbling connection between all of us. For, at least from the perspective of the community of all living things, humans urgently need to face up to our responsibility as the most dangerous and destructive of all predators.

Respecting Life

A ritual of respect for all those who have lived and are living in the Umfolozi area set the tone for our time in this wilderness — sharing the scent of a traditional African herb as the smouldering leaves are passed around. Before this ritual a talk on safety — how to walk close together, how to draw attention without shouting or talking, how signs to stop or retreat or make a detour must immediately be obeyed. And a moving reminder that during the next few days *we* are the visitors, entering one of the few remaining areas where these wild creatures are allowed to walk only on their own trails. Throughout the five days, whenever we see an animal in the distance our guides go out of their way to prevent the animals from being disturbed — no walking close to take a touristy picture. When we walk we are encouraged to be silent, for the human voice travels remarkably far in this environment.

We are encouraged not to look only for the Big Five. Every creature we encounter — dung beetles having a ball in mountains of elephant or rhino leftovers; shy spiders ("solifugids" — fugitives from the sun) running around the campfire at night; tree scorpions huddled in their tree-holes; birds of prey circling in the blue sky; little birds and butterflies darting between the bushes; different trees — each are given their name; each little string in the web of life is carefully described.

At night we use only as much wood as we need, far less than our vulnerable selves are inclined to want. In the morning we literally leave no visible human traces. Our droppings remain safely buried in private holes behind a bush or a tree — "gifts to renew the earth . . . it is all part of the cycle of life". At every temporary campsite, once the ash has been mixed with sand and strewn in different places, Bruce is the last to leave, carefully "sweeping the dining room" with a branch.

These practical expressions of respect for the environment and non-human life are important in themselves. Being encouraged to tread softly on the naked skin of an African wilderness invited us to walk less wastefully upon our return to clothed city living. Furthermore, there is the potential for this respect to reverberate through that part of the web where human life is found. For once one recovers an almost-childlike wonder at a dung beetle or an elephant, it becomes rather problematic to reduce the life of a fellow human being to being a "peeler" or a "screw" or a "terrorist". Once a sense of the underlying connectedness of all life is recognised, once *this* sense of inclusive, interdependent community is grasped, it becomes more difficult to remain blinkered by an impoverished sense of exclusively being "Protestant" or "Catholic", "Republican" or "Loyalist".

However, one of the reasons why it remains so difficult to unscatter our sense of community, to see beyond and below the blinkers, is because our senses are clogged, literally and figuratively, by the smog of city living, by the busy-ness of competing and surviving in the jungle of "civilisation".

Coming to Our Senses

First you dig a hole in the sand with your hands. Then you wait for the water to seep, gather and clear, slowly . . . miraculously. Cup by cup, carefully, a bucket is filled and then carried to the camp-site. Wood is gathered — twigs to get the fire going, thicker branches for heat. Once a little plateau of sand is crafted to protect the underlying roots and grass, the fire can be lit. A kettle is filled and placed above the flames. You wait and wait for the water to boil, smelling the wood burn, moving with the shifting breeze to avoid the smoke in your eyes. But there is no real hurry — you carry no watch, there is not much else to do. How refreshingly different are the slowness, the smells, the sounds, the textures and even the taste of this simple cup of tea or coffee from the usual instant, rushed experience back home.

The time in Umfolozi was indeed a wake-up call to one's senses — listening to the chorus of night and day sounds in an African wilderness, wondering at the abundance of stars, lying on your back in cool river water after a long walk in the heat, wiping your bum with grass, feeling hurrying hordes of belligerent ants, hungry after two days of rain and clouds, experiment with the taste of your toes.

It was also a time to come to one's senses — drinking in tranquillity and beauty, cherishing uninterrupted moments by yourself, just being. A time, if fully lived, which encourages one to be sensitive. A time to come

more alive to the deep, unifying meaning captured in
the following poem by Pablo Neruda:

Too Many Names

Mondays are meshed with Tuesdays
And the week with the whole year.
Time cannot be cut
With your exhausted scissors,
And all the names of the day
Are washed out in the waters of the night.

No-one can claim the name of Pedro,
Nobody is Rosa or Maria,
All of us are dust or sand,
All of us are rain under rain.
They have spoken to me of Venezuelas,
Of Chiles and Paraguays;
I have no idea what they are saying.
I know only the skin of the earth
And I know it is without a name . . .

Quoted in John O'Donohue, *Eternal Echoes* (Bantam Books, 2000, p. 18).

The few days that our diverse group got to know a little
more intimately the skin of that part of the earth which
first saw humans walking upright, before the culture of
naming began to blind us to the fact that, ultimately,
"All of us are dust or sand; *All of us* are rain under rain",
thus issued a profound invitation. An invitation that
challenges all scatterlings to become more awake to our
(human) connectedness and respectfully to nurture the
life in which we share. An invitation to say, with apolo-
gies to Neruda:

No-one can claim the name of Paddy or Brit,
   Protestant or Catholic, nationalist or unionist,
   loyalist or republican . . .
No-one can claim the name of Afrikaner or Afri-
   can, Coloured or Indian,
Nobody is taig or fenian,
Nobody is prod or screw or peeler . . .
Nobody is Boer or Kaffir, Bushie or Coolie . . .
Nobody is Green or Orange,
Nobody is White or Black, Brown or Yellow,
All of us
Are dust or sand,
All of us
ALL OF US
are rain under rain.

They have spoken to me of Irelands,
Of Great Britains and Ulsters,
They have also spoken to me of South Africas,
Of homelands and Bantustans — of Ciskeis and
   Transkeis, of Bophuthatswanas and Vendas, of
   KwaZulus and KwaNdebeles . . .
I have no idea what they are saying.
I know only the skin of the earth
And I know it is without a name.

Though the invitation to unscatter was inspired by Umfolozi's wildness, it was coloured by a country that,
nearly ten years after the dawning of political freedom, is
still struggling to emerge from the ravages of apartheid
— a system which has aptly been described as "one of the
twentieth century's most devastating experiments in the
denial of our common humanity" (Nadine Gordimer).

Noticing this shadow hanging over the beauty of that wilderness brings me, in closure, to another meaningful coincidence that prophetically took place on the day before we began to face in Umfolozi the legacy of the Troubles. The appropriate location for this coincidence was Kaya Mandi township, a stone's throw from the beauty of Stellenbosch, though in its poverty a world apart.

Returning from a disturbing walkabout through rows and rows of "shacks" (little tin-roofed dwellings, lining the highway almost all the 40-odd kilometres from Cape Town airport), we were given an unexpected performance by a newly formed local dance and drama group. Soon the dust was rising from the floor of the rundown community hall, as a "lion" and a "tiger", in tattered T-shirts, were circling each other, growling and snarling to the beat of an African drum. As the first imaginary drop of blood was spilt, the rolling and struggling on the ground seized immediately and a quarrel began. "Why did you spill my blood!?" raged the tiger. "This is MY blood!" countered the angry lion. Then, after a few similar dead-end exchanges, a sudden pause . . . and with the dawn of smiling white teeth on glistening black faces they at last came to their senses: "We are brothers! Our blood is the same."

Ian White

*Ian White was born in Newtownards in 1959 and was a
community worker in East Belfast before moving to Dublin in
1984. Since then Ian has worked with Focus Point, VSI and
Co-operation Ireland before joining Glencree as chief executive
in 1994. Ian is now developing his own training and consultancy business. He is married to Helen and they have four
sons, Rory, Owen, Jack and Ross.*

A S A YOUTH WORKER ON THE Newtownards Road, I
first visited Glencree in 1981 with a group of young
people who had never been across the border. Being
from a loyalist background, they were quite anxious
about what they would experience. The accommodation
at Glencree was extremely basic but the welcome was
warm from both paid and volunteer staff. I cannot remember exactly how many young people were in the
group but I do know that I returned home to East Belfast
with one group member less than I started with. This
young man was so taken by Glencree that he, being un-
employed and with no immediate need to return home,
decided to stay for a day or two more. This day or two
turned out to be six weeks as he overcame his reservations about the south and found new friends in the volunteers at Glencree.

I visited Glencree again a few times with a range of
groups, both cross-community and single identity be-

tween 1981 and 1985. At this point, I was providing voluntary work experience for young people from disadvantaged backgrounds in Ireland, north and south. The idea was that by working together the young people would build relationships with each other and come to understand that while they came from different backgrounds, their differences were enriching rather than threatening. By and large, this objective was achieved and a major factor was clearly the environment within which they working. This Glencree environment was uniquely supportive and extremely special for the young people. Most of the group had never had any great travel opportunities, so the volunteer team in a way brought the world to them through its multinational composition. The young people were included in the life of the centre and people at Glencree appeared to take what they had to say seriously. As a staff member working with the young people I came to value Glencree as a valuable resource for this type of work. Glencree owes much to both International Voluntary Service and Voluntary Service International for providing several hundred volunteers to work on manual projects around the centre.

It had been a few years since I had visited Glencree and in 1988 I attended a conference in Strasbourg. The conference was hosted by Service Civil International and by chance I met a former Glencree volunteer from Belgium, Wannes Van Stappen. (Johnny Walker in English!) Wannes had been a volunteer in Glencree for two years and when we visited the centre together in 1989 we speculated and dreamed about its potential as a place to build peace. Little did I know that I was to be invited to join the council of Glencree in 1991.

After three years on the council, in 1994 we decided that the appointment of a full-time Director was required in order to take Glencree forward and realise its potential in terms of peace building. As no one else could be found at the time, I was offered and accepted this position and another part of my journey with Glencree started.

The first activity for which I was responsible was a public talk on the peace process by John Hume. We had no suitable space in Glencree so we hosted this event in Jury's Hotel. Some 250 people attended and this provided much encouragement to all of us who were working to develop Glencree. Later that year, Chris McGimpsey addressed the Annual General Meeting in the Forge at the centre. With support from Atlantic Philanthropies, we were able to start a programme of facilitating political dialogue between members of all political parties in Ireland, north and south, and Britain. A grant from the Department of Foreign Affairs allowed capital improvements at the centre to commence with the fitting of new windows and the replacement of floors and roof. I remain grateful to the Office of Public Works for their ongoing support with maintenance and development of the building complex. Support from the Joseph Rowntree Charitable Trust allowed the appointment of an education programme worker in 1996.

Having initiated a new programme direction and having re-established the facilities in Glencree for use in peace-building, our attention turned to agreeing the core values of the organisation. It was agreed that pluralism and inclusivity would underpin all Glencree work and that an approach which is non-judgemental was an important prerequisite for engaging in peace-building work. These values are still as important to Glencree today as they were in 1994. Of course, just as these values create difficulty sometimes for our programme participants, they also represent a challenge to paid and volunteer staff at Glencree who must welcome everyone equally. It is through such challenges that understanding and tolerance are developed.

Reality in the voluntary sector is that funding is always an issue. There is a constant need to find funds at the same time as you deliver programmes. For Glencree it is no different. New and creative ways had to be found to secure the resources which were required to support a rapidly growing organisation. Grants from government and from voluntary trusts, while of critical importance, were no longer sufficient to support the ongoing work of the organisation. With the active support of our new President Alfie Kane, the Glencree Business Club was formed in 1998. This initiative created a mechanism for the business community to support the building of peace as well as providing an opportunity to become involved in the peace process.

In my decade as Chief Executive of Glencree, there were many privileges bestowed upon me. It was truly an honour to have listened to so many people's stories of their experiences of the conflict. Victims/survivors, former combatants, politicians and many more found it possible to tell their stories at Glencree. I was honoured to have heard many of them and as they humbled, angered, inspired and at times confused me, I grew in my understanding of the needs of peace-building.

Outside the programme participants, Glencree also played host to a wide range of well-known guests from Ireland and further afield. The then Secretary of State for Northern Ireland, Mo Mowlam, and the then Prime Minister of Canada, Jean Chrétien, were two of the first internationally recognisable figures to visit Glencree. Both of them did much through their visits to add momentum to the development of the programmes and facilities of Glencree. There were many other such visitors, however: former South African President F.W. De Klerk and the then Vice Chair of the South African TRC Alex Borraine are just two of a number of keynote speakers at what has become the Annual Glencree Summer School. Government ministers from Ireland and Britain, the leadership of the Liberation Tigers of Tamil Eelam, Senior Israeli and Palestinian politicians and many leaders and scholars from all over the world have honoured Glencree with their participation.

In a most significant event, HRH The Prince of Wales and Minister for Foreign Affairs, Brian Cowen, both made conciliatory remarks as they officially opened The Bridge (known still to many as the barracks). Perhaps one of the most profound discussions which I experienced at Glencree involved both men in dialogue with a group of Glencree programme participants. During this discussion HRH The Prince of Wales spoke of how it was forgiveness that sustained him when his uncle was assassinated. I wished then and still do that these remarks had been heard in a more public arena.

Glencree has been true to its values and through its programmes has demonstrated a willingness to take risks for peace. It has responded positively to the opportunities and challenges of peace-building in an ever-changing context. While it remains focused on its work within and between Ireland and Britain, it is now being drawn to working and sharing experiences with people in other conflict situations around the world. There are many people to acknowledge in the story of the last ten years of Glencree. They know who they are. They are all of the participants on our programmes, Council members, paid and volunteer staff, members of the Glencree Business Club, the British and Irish Governments, a range of diplomatic missions to Ireland, other partner NGOs and the many others who provided expertise, time and encouragement. Individually, none of us holds a monopoly on wisdom and yet collectively we can modestly say "we contributed to the building of peace".

I hope and trust that the Glencree experience has been as significant for our programme participants as it was for the Chief Executive.